THE BILLION BUCK BUSINESS

BECOME A BUSINESS DEVELOPER WITH VENTESKRAFT MEDIA

MAHIN BS
CEO and Co founder, Venteskraft

INDIA • SINGAPORE • MALAYSIA

Notion Press

Old No. 38, New No. 6
McNichols Road, Chetpet
Chennai - 600 031

First Published by Notion Press 2020
Copyright © Mahin BS 2020
All Rights Reserved.

ISBN 978-1-64783-861-4

This book has been published with all efforts taken to make the material error-free after the consent of the author. However, the author and the publisher do not assume and hereby disclaim any liability to any party for any loss, damage, or disruption caused by errors or omissions, whether such errors or omissions result from negligence, accident, or any other cause.

While every effort has been made to avoid any mistake or omission, this publication is being sold on the condition and understanding that neither the author nor the publishers or printers would be liable in any manner to any person by reason of any mistake or omission in this publication or for any action taken or omitted to be taken or advice rendered or accepted on the basis of this work. For any defect in printing or binding the publishers will be liable only to replace the defective copy by another copy of this work then available.

This book is dedicated to everyone who wants to break free from the shackles of traditional education and the monotony of the 9-5 life; to everyone who wants to take life by the lapels and become financially independent; and to everyone who wants to choose a unique path in life, not a conventional one.

CONTENTS

Acknowledgements		7
Preface		9
1.	How I Became a Business Developer	11
2.	How I Made My First Student a Successful Freelance Business Developer	15
3.	Who Can Become a Business Developer?	17
4.	What is The Future for Business Developers?	25
5.	Lifestyle of a Business Developer	33
6.	How I Got 100 Multinational Companies as My Clients	37
7.	Advantages of Having a Youtube Channel	43
8.	Cold Calling: How & Why	51
9.	Personal Branding	59
10.	Influencer Marketing	65
11.	Getting the Right Mentors	71
12.	Appointing Employees	79
13.	What Does it Feel Like to Have a Million Dollars!	85
14.	How Google Adwords Work	91
15.	Use Facebook to Your Advantage	99
16.	Power of Economics	105
17.	Gain Exposure of Different Markets	111
18.	What Makes or Breaks a Company	115
19.	Artifical Intelligence	121
20.	Do or Die Co-Founder	129
21.	Digital Marketing Tools That a Business Developer Must Know.	133

Contents

22.	Different Business Development Strategies.	165
23.	How to Get Rich by Affiliate Marketing?	175
24.	Importance of Dropshipping.	181
25.	E-Commerce Business.	185
26.	Dealing With Criticism as a Business Developer?	189
27.	MBA Versus Business Development Programme	191

ACKNOWLEDGEMENTS

I would like to extend my gratitude to everyone who has been a part of this book, without whose assistance and guidance the successful completion of the book would not have been possible.

Their contributions are appreciated and gratefully acknowledged. Thank You.

I would also like to thank everyone who loved my first book. It motivated me to write the second one.

PREFACE

In every chapter of this book, mention has been made of everything that is valuable for any person embarking on the journey of financial independence.

I had to take charge of my life at a very young age and hence I realized that though traditional education is important, it is in no way necessary to be successful in life. I realized that a person who doesn't get straight A's at academics can still make it big in life. There are a lot of wonderfully talented people bogged down by the idea of having a heavy and flashy CV, instead of having skills that actually work.

Once I found my way into financial independence, I decided to make a difference and help others who want to make a difference too. I have been a Business Developer for a long time now and have guided a lot of people in their journey of being one too.

People know a lot about business but most do not know about Business Development and how inevitably important it is to have this strategy in place for long-lasting success.

Being experienced at the science of Business Development and being aware of the importance of it, I was motivated to teach more and more people about which I do, every day.

I had to write this book so that the message spreads across amongst Businesses on how important Business Development is and for people looking for a career that makes them big money on how being is Business Developer is the way to go.

HOW I BECAME A BUSINESS DEVELOPER

//Sometimes a choice of career is an intensively planned out path,
Sometimes it just comes as a random thought that stayed. //

Mine is the latter and this is how. Right after passing the 12th, in the year 2012, just like most kids that age, I was confused about "What Now?" I had never firmly decided during my school what I wanted to do, hence I was in a state of sheer dilemma. So as fancy as it sounds, I chose to do my bachelors in Aerospace Engineering from Alliance University, Bangalore.

But the curious kid in me was always roused with questions about how the college managed to attract a good number of students, especially considering that ours was the first batch; how have so many people learnt about this institution, with each student paying around a hefty INR 1.25 to 1.5 lakh per year. I pondered and realized that I was one of their clients too, I had been attracted too and the institution was just like any other company in the corporate.

Thereafter I met one of my mentors, who is the Marketing Head of a leading Multinational Company in Malaysia. I hurled my rally of questions at him about how these people cram in a decent count of clients and a humongous quantity of money. He educated me about the difference between Traditional and Digital Marketing and I learnt the basics of Digital Marketing from him via Skype and thereafter I learnt Business Development myself.

During the 2nd year of college I helped a friend, who owned a hardware shop at Dubai, with getting clients using Search Engine Optimization. We got positive results and he shared a section of profit with me. Alongside this I was also trading in stocks.

However, then life took another road and I met with an accident on November 28th 2013, which was my birthday. This is as funny as relatable. During my immature years where I was hitting adolescence, I drove rash to get an adrenaline rush. However, my car didn't quite agree and toppled over, and then the insurance company didn't agree either and rejected my claim by quoting obscure reasons. Anyway I managed to convince them and could get the claim for my car which is when I realized I had the skill of convincing and which is when I also realized that rejecting claims on no absolute grounds was a common practice of the insurance companies.

So I started searching through the complaint forum on Google to find the other claims that had been rejected and people had complained about. I found out quite a few, communicated with those people and made a deal with them of getting their claims done in exchange of commission.

My first client was a Cardiac Arrest patient and wanted to get a medical insurance, His claim was rejected just because he had visited some other hospital, I helped him through in getting a claim worth 5 lakh INR and I charged a commission of 1 lakh using which I paid my college fee fortunately in which I had a 50% scholarship owing to my 98% score in the 12th.

I was pursuing these little ventures because my family had become bankrupt after my father's business in Dubai faced quandary and I was the only person earning for my family prior to which my father was the only person earning our bread. Little did I know that these will integrate to shape my life and make me who I am today.

After I earned the commission for getting that patient the insurance claim I realized how powerful the internet is. I could reach out to strangers who shared the common problem as mine and provide them help in exchange of money using which I could help my family in return.

People do know that internet is a great discovery, but not everyone knows how it can be used to their advantage. Not only has the internet knit the world closer and made it a smaller place, but it has also widened the realm of opportunities. From making the very daunting task of communication incredibly easy and getting the news from anywhere around the globe to spread in the blink of an eye with almost everything we want just a click away. The social, economic, political and cultural aspects of the globe have been reshaped. The web is a plethora of facts and statistics; even the paperback books have given way to e-books, this infinite resource just needs to be tapped wisely. Can we even imagine our lives without the internet?

In the meanwhile, I happened to read the biography of Steve Jobs written by Walter Isaacson wherein I was marveled at the story of a student who was forever interested in electronics switching over to liberal arts and then dropping out of college and joining the Hippie Commune where he primarily grew apples and after a series of events becoming the founder of one of the biggest technical giants ever, Apple. The rest is history.

Furthermore, I would always wonder how Bill Gates made the whopping amount of money that he did, by building the largest software business ever (with his partner Paul Allen) that too in an era of Traditional Marketing. It is not a secret that he is an inspiration to millions of people.

And now with internet having taken over the entire face of Earth, how could Marketing have been left behind. Digital Marketing has been winning over Traditional Marketing by a gargantuan margin since its advent. The surge of Business Development has grown the reach of products exponentially. This is a gadget driven, tech savvy era where almost everything is facilitated online and it is without a doubt the most productive means to advertise your business because the power shift has caused more and more people to move online via social media. According to Google, companies using Business Development strategies have a 2.8 times better revenue growth expectancy. As brands are gradually realizing the importance of Business Development they are becoming super active with their hunt of people who possess skills in Business Development which is why I am writing this book.

I started my journey as you may have known by now as a freelance Business Developer and now, have around 150-175 clients all over the world. It took a lot of learning and dedication to reach a place where I want to and am able to educate more people about the scope of Internet and of Business Development, and what wonders can be reaped if these are used in a right manner.

Nowadays people spend most of the day with their eyes fixated on the screens of their digital devices while they browse through the internet. Companies and brands are on a massive lookout for people who can procure the maximum out of this using the finest skills. I want to train as many people as I can and help them to benefit from this and it needs to be propagated that one can make freelance business development an active source of ample income while being your own boss without having to work for anyone 9-5 or an additional source of income even if you want to continue with your current job. You can learn and earn as a freelance

Business Developer even if you are a student and lighten the burden on your parents or get an extra pocket money. You just need to work hard, smart and have faith.

So let us embark on our journey to making the best out of Business Development.

HOW I MADE MY FIRST STUDENT A SUCCESSFUL FREELANCE BUSINESS DEVELOPER

I know we live in a world full of make believers and I know prudent people demand facts and figures, not tales and opinions. That is why I am citing this journey of my first Business Development student who is also my close friend and how I played a major role in helping him become a successful full time freelance Business Developer.

This dates back to the year 2017 when a close friend of mine, Rahul Rajeev, was pursuing his Bachelors in Engineering from Vellore Institute of Technology, Vellore. He was doing some sundry business and also looking for additional part time work to widen his base for income. That is when I educated him about Business Development and trained him in the same the best that I could in my capacity about the tools that are deployed in the practice of Business Development. He had absolutely no prior knowledge or background in Business Development. After ample trainings from my end and consistent hard work from his, he got an offer to undertake performing Business Development for a supermarket.

So, his first client was a supermarket which was a good prospect. As mentioned in the previous chapter, internet has become omnipotent and everything we want is just a click away. Supermarkets have to face a turmoil in keeping up with the developing times with the coming up of the online stores with all different kinds offers and services. In the said scenario strategic marketing, specifically Business Development is the need of the hour because even if the Supermarkets can't go digital, at least their marketing can. He used a variety of tools and strategies that suited the situation well and managed to get the supermarket a continuous inflow of clients. And that is how he became a full time Business Developer.

That's how a person who was nowhere academically related to even the ABCs of Business Development kick started his career in the same and anyone who works smartly in the right direction can gain an expertise in this field.

Thereafter he started marketing online and got a client from software company from Malaysia. After learning the potential of his skill and foreseeing the prospective fruits of continuing the same, he hired some two to three employees to manage his client. See, that is the power of belief and hard work; hard work in the right dimensions that in a considerably little span of time, a person who was looking to be hired for part time work started hiring other people to work for him.

Soon, he started attracting clients from the US, Malaysia and India, thus expanding his client base overseas. In the meantime, he was also managing the Social Media pages for some companies which thereafter showed an appreciable growth in their business, noticing which other neighboring companies also reached out to him to take up business development for their businesses. And that is how with my training and his consistent hard and smart work, he built himself as brand in business development.

For things to fit into the frame better, Rahul's parents were in Dubai, so we happened to visit Dubai. It is no hidden fact that Dubai is a premium ranked hub for business. Dubai has emerged as a global hub, showed by **Knight and Frank in their Hub Report 2015**. According to **CBRE reports,** more than half of the biggest global conglomerates operating offices are present in the high powered city of Dubai. Rather quickly, it has established its reputation as a vibrant and diverse destination offering quality hospitality, first-class infrastructure, and range of attractions. Hence, there is a huge number of companies on a lookout for Business Developers to increase the potential of their business. So, we talked to various companies and tried to convince them to take our services. We were successful in convincing them and owing to a huge export and import business that happens to and fro Dubai, we involved ourselves in the import and export business as well.

WHO CAN BECOME A BUSINESS DEVELOPER?

What is Business Development?

Business Development is aimed at creating a long term value to the organization which, in simpler terms is achieved by ideas, initiatives, strategic decision, building relationships and activities to make the business better. To make a business better is to increase the revenue, generate optimum profit, maintain positive cash flow, expand the scope of business and increase the reach and base of clients.

What does a Business Developer do?

A business developer creates opportunities and roadmap for potential growth and supports and monitors their implementations and takes a feedback from specialist functions to assure if the organization can implement the opportunity effectively and successfully. He works to attract new customers to the products and services of a business and to increase the consumption of the existing customers by advertising, cold calling, networking and other means.

Why is Business Development Important?

No businesses keep running and running smoothly on their own. There are several back-end works which are necessary for any company to survive, hence it is very important to have business developers in the team to handle bringing client to the counter with the expertise they bring to the table. Business Development is the link between the external components of the company like potential partnerships, new business opportunities, client relations to the internal components of company like marketing, sales, product development and services.

Furthermore, if one looks around, he may find a plethora of opportunities to take benefit from but just like not every shoe fits everyone, every opportunity cannot be promising and fruitful to every business. It is very important to identify the product of your company and what all it specifically needs, to grow and thrive amidst rising competition every day given the investment and opportunities that a company has. It is also very important to identify the conductors of your business and also that of the market, competitors and customers because those are the major factors in the business environment. To carry out this extensive research, a Business Development team is needed.

Aside from creating new products, tapping new opportunities and creating new clients and customers, it is perhaps of utmost necessity for any company to retain its old and current customers because customers are the building blocks of any business.

Though not exhaustive but these, to list a few, are the reasons why companies hire and should hire a team for Business Development and to have the Business Development strategy in place.

WHAT HAPPENS IN THE ABSENCE OF STRATEGIC BUSINESS DEVELOPMENT?

A proper strategy is very pivotal to be successful in life. If we do not know what to do next or how to do it, our life will become a mess of all tasks placed disorderly. Similarly, if there isn't a strategy in place, it becomes very difficult for any business to function, flourish and prosper. A set of guidelines to carry out the capital rationing, project selection, marketing and daily operations etc. is the backbone of any firm. Without having a coherent objective, there won't be an identifiable vision for future which in turn will lead to poor focus in achieving corporate goals and framing business plans to grow the business and bring sustained success to the organization.

Amid the lack of a proper business development strategy, the mistakes of improper allocation of resources are bound to happen wherein the available resources are consumed by a non-profitable or a not so profitable venture.

A lack of proper strategy also leads to lack of articulate communication within the organization and with the external links of the organization. Miscommunication causes misinterpretation, in every walk of life and can wreak havoc for your organization. Hence, it is crucial to have a strategy oriented Business Development team to achieve the organization's mission and goal.

ROLE OF A BUSINESS DEVELOPER

As foresaid, a business developer's role is crucial for any business and it requires a lot of investment because he works to improve the market position of the company while also providing with financial growth and generating consistent revenue and cash inflow. The business developer helps achieve long term goals, studies and keeps extensive knowledge of the marketplace in order to make the best of the feasible business opportunities, maintains and builds customer relations, closes final deals and negotiates them.

Business Development managers rely on knowledge of market and the business, experience and strategies to help a business grow to its full potential and to improve the efficiency and sustainability of the company.

The following skills are necessary for a Business Developer to produce positive outcomes:

BE A GOOD SALESPERSON

Being a good salesperson is the prime quality that a business developer needs to have. Since the building blocks of any business are the clients and the customers, it is but natural that to survive and thrive a business needs to expand on its client and customer base, for which selling them the product and service is very crucial. With the infinite options available in the market, aside from making your service attractive with respect to quality, being able to convince the customer about it is a task. That is where a skilled Business Developer steps in. He has to make the sale and he does it by cold calling, networking emailing, advertising and proper marketing to generate interest of the potential clients and widen the client share balloon and maintain the existing ones. It is very important to have good marketing in place, because after all that is what is going to bring in the customers which will eventually improve the bottom line.

They need to identify potential customers, present to them, convince them and ultimately convert them into clients and help to grow business in future.

The Business Developer will also help manage existing clients and ensure they stay satisfied and positive. They call on clients, make presentations on solutions and services that meet or predict their clients' future needs.

COMMUNICATION AND INTERPERSONAL SKILLS

A lack of proper communication can lead to a whole lot of mess and problems. We all are aware what ruination miscommunication can create, even in your personal life. A good business developer must be able to communicate to the team the feasible idea for the project to be undertaken, the strategy for business growth and to communicate to the customer the features of products and services. Only then can any business function. He must have good communication skills, to present, assert to and convince all the stakeholders involved. He must also be able to cold call prospects with confidence in order to gain new clients.

The Business Developer must develop a rapport with new clients, and set targets for sales and provide support that will improve the relationship. Also, it's a requirement to grow and retain existing clients and customers by presenting new solutions and services to clients.

The fluency of language and clarity of thought are mandatory to good communication skills and a business developer equipped with the same shall bring laurels to the company.

NEGOTIATION AND COLLABORATIVE SKILLS

A business developer must know how to work with teams, it isn't a one-man parade and collaborative skills are of utmost importance. A business developer should be able to collaborate with multiple parties; outside and inside the organization.

He should be able to build relationships, influence, manage conflicts and navigate to get things done. Also, he will need to be tactful, discreet and diplomatic. He is required to know when to compromise and when to not, to achieve the set goals. This is all that a business developer will need to maintain and build long lasting relationships with clients and customers.

Moreover, smart negotiation skills, one can only imagine, are how important in every walk of life, let alone business development. A business developer needs to have informed ability to negotiate to close deals and help price the products and services at the optimal number.

In order to persuade and convince the prospects on buying him or his team member into doing what should be done, a business developer will need to win their heart, mind soul and trust. A people's person is the best tool to have, to grow, maintain leverage the people network.

A business developer works with a team to plan proposal, approaches and pitches. He works to develop proposals that address the client's needs, concerns, and objectives.

He must handle objections by clarifying, emphasizing agreements and working through differences to a positive conclusion and develop and use a variety of methods to persuade or negotiate appropriately.

PROJECT MANAGEMENT AND DECISION MAKING SKILLS

How should a business developer deal with the people and process involved with business development?

Good Business Development Managers are exactly that; Good Managers! They are required to be able to set SMART goals, plan and manage the new and ongoing projects. They also manage the risks involved with the projects; calculate budgets, rations them across projects taken up and also manage the costs, time and teams working on the projects.

Businesses, whether private or public operate in an ever changing, dynamic environment. Organizations have recognized the need to develop and adopt operations to meet evolving market environment and objectives. This calls for a constant need of managers and decision makers who can take quick, strategic and feasible decisions and manage them well.

A business developer needs to be a good manager to be able to focus on the development of capacity and capability that improve the output rather than focus on just the output.

He also needs to initiate projects by taking into consideration the externalities(cannibalization), i.e. the impact of a new venture on the existing ones; avoiding duplication, overlapping, conflicts in the demand of resources and redundant changes that undo the benefits instead of bringing about positive changes.

RESEARCH AND STRATEGIC SKILLS

Research and Development make to the income statement of any business as one of the most important components. Apart from that, even the government allocates a part of the budget every year, to research and development which obviously signifies how important are the research skills for growth of company and country alike.

Market research is crucial when launching product, improving the existing product and getting ahead of the competitors in the market;

because it provides with all the data and knowledge necessary to make better and optimal business decision.

It helps understand the customer better. The theory of demand as stated by economics mentions that a consumer's preferences and expectations is one of the important components in deciding the demand for a product and service. A study of the nature of customers and potential customers hence comes handy when tailoring the products to make them better to meet customer needs better, which is important to compete with the competitors in the market.

In the words of **Hilary Mason,** "As your competitors learn more, you'll need to learn too." This is absolutely true. As much as the business developers are required to know the customer they are also required to know the competitor because everyone's here to "beat the market." Knowing the competitor and how they approach the market, what their strengths and weaknesses are will help design products ahead of them.

Research is also important to track the benchmark which is in turn important to accumulate profits more than the market benchmark.

We've seen market giants like Kodak and Nokia suffer the hit of insufficient research and inability to adapt to the changing market needs and environment. Hence, it's very important to maintain ample research and flexibility to be able to adapt to the upcoming and ongoing changes and it is very important for a business developer to have skills to conduct market research efficiently.

COMPUTER SKILLS

Be it business development or any other job, being acquainted with how to use a computer is the basic requirement. Although a Business developer might not be needed to be well versed with the programming, the data science, the machine learning or how AI works; but he should have high competency with how basic applications like Microsoft word, Microsoft PowerPoint etc. work.

Given that in this era communication, research and analysis all depends upon computers; the knowledge of computers becomes all the more crucial to be known by a business developer.

A lack of computer knowledge can really lead to inefficiencies and inability to reach the true potential along with sending out a signal that the business developer is unable to keep up with the times which of course doesn't happen to be a good signal.

BUSINESS INTELLIGENCE

Smart work over Hard work is the mantra that every successful person has been following. Knowing all about the business he engages in, is obviously an unavoidable skill that a business developer must have but so as far as the knowledge of one's own project is important, the knowledge of the competitors' will only do more good by making one aware of their competitive advantage.

Collecting, analyzing and staying updated with the current data are a part of business intelligence that a business developer will need to maintain. Also, analytical skills come in handy when dealing with market statistics and trends. Knowing the size and dynamics of marketplace can ensure an edge over the others.

Hence, apart from general intelligence, a business developer must also be business intelligent.

All in all, for a business development manager to stand out, he must always be on a lookout for learning more and stay updated with the latest business and economic issues in the industry. Sales management, marketing, strategy and planning can be used as strengths to grow the business to prevent the hindrance in business growth from external and internal factors.

WHAT IS THE FUTURE FOR BUSINESS DEVELOPERS?

Through the last three chapters, we learnt what Business Development is all about, what skills are needed to become a business development manager and how one can go about becoming a successful business developer. I also shared my journey of becoming a successful business developer and how I helped one of my friends in becoming one too.

We also learnt that with the surge in the use of the internet, how business development can be the be all and end all in determining whether a business will thrive or not survive.

It is indeed evident that the scope for business development in the present is sky high making it one of the most lucrative, attractive and sought after career options, but I understand anything that seems too bright today might lose its shine over time. It is also possible that the now less supply, more demand interaction changes to a more supply, less demand interaction leaving people who learnt business development with no work and hence no means to make money.

So, in this chapter we will discuss about the future of business development industry and if is it worth it in the long term to pursue business development as a career option. Business Development is the best career choice these days and the scope of business development is endless and in this chapter I will explain to you each and every angle of what makes business development an ideal, lucrative, long term and reliable career choice. If you are already in this industry you will be able to relate and agree with me but if you are thinking about taking up business development as your career and sky rocket your income as an employee, a freelancer or a business owner; you have landed at the right place.

Given the dense population of the world, new opportunities are being created every minute and a new startup being ventured frequently, being shut even more frequently! Why? Because of the lack of strategies that are needed to convert an investment into an income generating medium!

A failure of planning is an evidence of a planning of failure, there can't be any rebuttals or debates on this fact.

A lack of proper marketing also has not so good consequences on the business. I mean obviously, how will people buy your services if they don't even know about you or your services? Why will people buy your services out of the others available even after they learn about them? That is where a business developer comes into picture, to provide a solution for these whys and how's!

Any person or group of people who have put their creative energy, intellectual energy, time and money into starting a business and carrying it forward wouldn't shy away from deploying one of the key drivers that is business development or would they? Nobody ever starts a start up to shut it down.

Coming back to the question of whether business development as a career is here to stay. Obviously YES! Will the population ever stop growing? Will the startups ever stop being taken up? Will the need for marketing ever disappear? NO! The digital skills are embedded in every era of our lives and the Internet and the Digital Era are here to stay.

Business Development skills are in serious demand and the skills gap is set to widen, the job and startup market is booming and brands are putting more of a focus on business development than ever before, are going to put even more focus on it in the coming years.

There is a plenty of room for people looking to enter the world of business development and related careers. At present, some of the most in-demand skills are content creation and curation, social media strategy, and analytics, which is great news for those who steer towards the creative, social and business end of the spectrum and serves as an evidence that business development as a career option is here to stay.

Use of mobile, electronic devices and internet is on the rise with a graph that only goes upwards. Business Development strategies and Digital Marketing strategies affect buying behaviors and decisions of consumers. People spend time on their mobile devices such as smartphones, tablets or laptops more than ever.

Brands need to connect with customers in real time and increase the reach to improve the conversion rate through all of these devices by creating the right social media campaigns, e-commerce, and display advertising. The way that people interact with a brand through mobile

apps or websites has been changing the nature of marketing and proving to be a boon for the brands and in turn for the business developers.

You see how this forms a cycle? A business developer helps the company; the company deploys more services from the business developer.

One of the big reasons we are seeing business development get demanded so much is not only because of the adoption of new technologies, but also because the web is getting saturated, there are approximately 1,806,360,110 websites on the web.

A GLIMPSE INTO THE FUTURE

The Economist Intelligence Unit asked 499 (one can't help but think they were aiming for 500) Chief Marketing Officers and Senior Marketing Execs about how they saw marketing evolving, and also conducted some in-depth, one on one interviews with CMOs from leading brands such as Unilever and JPMorgan Chase.

They were looking to find out what key technologies and trends will drive change in the marketing industry over the next four years, and the results make for interesting reading."

Robert Allen from Smart Insights thinks that business developers will have full control of customer experience of the products and services of a company in the near future. According to The Economist Intelligent Unit's research, by 2020 top 3 hottest trends for business developers will impact the organizations and businesses.

These are **mobile devices** and **networks, Personalization Technologies** and the **Internet of Things.** The key channels for measuring marketing efforts will still be **social media, web** and **mobile apps.**

In the future, traditional business models will leave their place to the platforms that companies can directly connect with customers. In the coming years, more than 50% of Global 2000 will see most of their businesses depend upon their ability to create products, services and experiences that are digitally driven and enhanced.

Business development does not only mean digital marketing and technology, and it will eventually affect every industry for many and many years to come. The companies should make preparations and be ready to adapt to the upcoming changes.

Forbes' **Adrian Gomez** discusses on the information about the constant change of business development in his article. Gomez suggests the businesses to leave behind outdated strategies and adopt innovative ones by telling stories, leveraging reviews and generating buzz with authenticity.

The scope of Business Development in the present is already HUGE! And it is only going to get bigger and bigger. *Already huge: 40% of US adults use voice search once per day. Going to get bigger: comScore estimates that 50% of ALL searches will be voice searches within the next 2 years." – Brian Dean Founder & CEO at Backlinko.*

Everyone in the country is preferring business development over everything else. Even the startups are launching their business via business development. This platform eases the process of every business.

It offers a wide range of economical, powerful and contemporary mechanisms and mediums of starting a business and its marketing. Every type of product and service is now opting for the option of business development. Because they know that this is the proven method to give a head start to your startup or boost your already established business.

Business Development as a career path is something that not many people take up intentionally but definitely has a hefty demand in the job sector and is very critical to any organization that wants to grow to the maximum potential. . A business developer is the only non-owner of a business who is the closest to the ownership of the business given that he supervises the planning, execution, marketing and operations of the business. It's not uncommon for an organization to move someone from their business development team to the project start-up team when they win a project, because everyone likes to continue winning. After all, they will be more intimately acquainted with the business program and model than anyone else. Working on proposals is a demanding and often stressful role. Many employers reward those who put in their time by helping them transition to other areas of the company rather than lose them to burnout.

If you happen to be someone who thrives in this role, there are opportunities at all stages of your career to advance to the highest levels of an organization and get handsome compensations and perks.

Will any organization ever let go of a person on this position given that he is basically responsible for the livelihood of the organization, knows the business model so close and has given positive results in the past? No way! So we again know now that business development as a career option is here to stay, for a very very long time!

At present, no industry is complete without incorporating business development into its working because that constitutes one of the first and critical steps and aspects in **starting and continuing a profit generating business.**

Business Development sets its footmark across business verticals drawing the best possible ROI and revenue for the business by chalking out possible business models and selecting the best one owing to experience and skill. This is the easiest and convenient method of creating and promoting specific products or services to respective target audience with limited resources and in a defined time frame efficiently. Thus we can consider business development as the best business practice for business optimization and also for business growth.

All most all the companies or businesses are making ways towards business development aiming quick and better results and higher profitability. As a result, there is a huge demand for business development professionals having skills and expertise in business development. Also, business development is one of the highest paid professions of all times concerning market demand.

Business Development is currently having a huge impact on both business and career. This is the cheapest mode of marketing and promoting goods/services to millions of people at a time. Almost all the business verticals are benefited with digital marketing.

Business Development eliminates all the drawbacks of traditional business method. Therefore, it is popular across the globe to an extent, where it has become difficult for any business to run without it. The flexibility and convenience of this potent tool allows the business organization to grab high return on investment and generate profits.

The crazy race of surviving and thriving within every small and big enterprises to establish rock-solid and on-line reputation and higher profitability, has led to plenty of job vacancies. There is a growing demand for certified business development professionals all over the world. Given that business development is one of the most crucial and in-demand job profiles available, especially at MSMEs & MNCs. and that people really cannot get just enough skilled business development professionals hence compensation hikes and job stability are more prominent in this field. If you were to work consistently and persistently, you would definitely go places with this position at hand.

Business development manager has various roles to play in the working of the business organization like financial planning, projections and budgets; marketing; data analysis; report writing; forecasting. It is extremely varied which is one of the reasons why you'd love it as there's potential for your holistic growth and you get to work on such diverse facets of the same business.

Another key aspects of the job of a business developer are to understand the process, analyze the ongoing process and accordingly pick the one to be taken up in future. If the business isn't performing well you have to figure out the 'why' and then have the 'know-how' to make it better. If the business is doing well, a business developer must pick the strong point and play on it to maintain the positive outcome and make them even better.

Every organization is always launching a new product or service, a business developer through their skills of identifying organizations and people who would be needing the new and not so well-known product or service and then making data-backed pitching to them through discussions and cold calling. Needless to say, if you are one of those very rare people with the right personality, temperament, and communication skills to perform this difficult role effectively, your salary potential will be huge because every company wanting to introduce a new technology or penetrate a new market has this problem. With a little savvy negotiation, you will end up pocketing a huge amount of money.

Furthermore, a business developer has to interface with the product development team and discuss with them about how to evolve the product in response to customer feedbacks and demands.

Depending on the state of the business and industry, that may be looking to sustain the current growth rate or bounce back from the losses. But growing a business takes significant strategy to ensure it has nabbing quality, lasting clients that take the business to the next level. And today's frequently changing business landscape can lay challenges in that path.

If the goal of a business, which why wouldn't be? Then, to stand the test of time and sustain success, the business organization would need to adopt leading industry and consumer trends for which it'll need to hire a business development manager.

The success as a business developer really depends on how you'll be able to handle, materialize and bring in more closures and once you are confident, The Sky Is the Limit!

LIFESTYLE OF A BUSINESS DEVELOPER

Before stepping into any career choice in the world; more than knowing what it is all about, it is also important to know how your life will be affected, both positively and negatively; after all that is something you'll engage yourself with, every waking day, for all your life to make yourself a living.

Through the course of last few chapters, we learnt the skills that a business developer needs to have for the tasks that he has to do. In this chapter we are going to take a look at what the lifestyle of a business developer is like.

As we read in the previous chapter, there is a multitude of tasks that a business developer has to perform every day; we surely can say that the lifestyle of a business developer is pretty dynamic. The day needs to be carefully planned in a target driven way that ensures that the demands of the clients be met and the daily tasks can be achieved in the most efficient manner and success can be delivered to the clients and to self as a winning business developer.

Since, the major part of the business development process is making hypotheses about what strategy to use and what plan of action to take; a business developer must spend a major chunk of his time in studying the market and the competitors, the new available resources, the resources about to be obsolete, the most appropriate methods and the list goes on. Hence, a business developer needs to keep up with what is happening outside everyday and spends some of his day reading news and blogs and the market.

Below are mentioned some of the tasks that a business developer is entrusted with and how each of them affects the daily life of a business developer.

NETWORKING AND BUILDING RELATIONSHIPS

A part of the day, every day, of a business developer will be devoted to communicating because developing long term and stable relationships is the lifeblood of the business development practice; after all it is people that make or break a business. A business developer therefore needs to send cold e-mails, make phone calls and hold meeting to communicate the company's value to the potential clients and customers.

GETTING THE DEALS AND CLOSING THEM

This goes without mentioning! After all, all this communication, research etc is being done to get business deals, right? Then, closing deals obviously becomes one of the most important tasks to be put in the list of daily targets to do because eventually the purpose of the entire business development is to get deals.

STUDYING THE TREND AND MAKING THE MOST OF IT

Business development professional needs to study the market, lay a hypothesis for future and also study how changes in other markets might trickle down to the market that the given company is dealing in. For instance, if there are technological advances happening, how it might affect the demand for the product that the given company is offering or how the technical advancement may positively or negatively affect the said company needs to be taken into account. Another instance is if the surge of online deliveries will affect the offline stores. Then based on the statistics and information collected he connects the dots and proposes a strategy and takes a decision that shall bear the most fruitful results.

COMPETITIVE INTELLIGENCE

The main motive of competitive intelligence is to develop a comparative advantage against your competitors. By this, I mean to say that by acquiring the relevant information as mentioned in the previous paragraph, a business developer can leverage it to the company's advantage by acting on the information before and better than the competitors. Therefore, it comes back to the point that a business developer must be deft at finding information, forecasting trends and acting on the same.

OWNING YOUR TIME

As a business developer to a company, you are going to receive tons and tons of inbound e-mails and calls from people who want to pitch their product to you. You will need to spend time going through these mails and make sure you stick to your deal and prioritize based on the same.

AN EYE TOWARDS EXIT

Sometimes companies are too focused on building big businesses that do not appropriately plan on the exit, if ever needed. Neither do they plan for a merger nor an acquisition, if any, might be needed in future. This is particularly important for companies looking to go liquid on their investments. Identifying potential exits for the startup and using Business Development as a means to develop a relationship is advantageous.

PRIORITIZE

With a vast variety of tasks being entrusted unto the business developer, a crazy amount of e-mails being received, a lot of research and planning being done; sometimes it becomes very important to prioritize the tasks because sometimes all can't be performed together or in a short time span. Therefore, it is indeed of utmost importance that a business developer plans his day based upon what task tops the priority and what task can be postponed to a later time.

A DAY IN THE LIFE OF A BUSINESS DEVELOPER

The day of a business developer starts quite early. This is because he needs to check headlines, catch up on news and read anything that could be relevant. Why? I have already mentioned the absolute necessity of being up-to-date with the news and the market. The business developer can accommodate his breakfast too during this time.

Next, he needs to share the information gathered early in the day and the inferences drawn via his business account or personal account to the people it is relevant to and then leave for the office.

After reaching the office, a business developer plans out his day per the pointers mentioned in the last few pages keeping priority in mind.

He then proceeds to check his e-mails and addresses those that require a quick response. The rest of the mails are moved to the daily "actions" list.

Thereafter, he speaks with the team and goes over the daily Key Performance Indicators. All of the above mentioned tasks must be completed by 9 AM.

After 9 AM, individual or group meetings are conducted to talk about the latest projects, the plan of action, the execution, the progress and the feedback on the same.

After the successful dissemination of the meeting, a business developer attends to clients on the outstanding issues and starts executing his daily "actions" list.

Thereafter, a considerable amount of time of 2 hours must be devoted to writing the action plan, execution plan, the blog posts and press releases.

Once the business developer has efficiently completed these tasks, he can catch up with his lunch and in the meantime also go through news, blog posts, Twitter, LinkedIn, Facebook and also chat with and chat with other professionals in the industry.

Then the business developer takes a stock of the client activities by looking at the analytics reports. This is done by going over the key metrics that are individualized for each client. This includes knowing what content has had the most attention and if the users have any questions that require answering. The analytics are also used to find out if there is something unexpected and gather insights on it. All of this also takes some 2 hours to complete.

After reading and scrutinizing the analytics report, the business developer addresses any tasks left out from the "actions" list and answers the remaining e-mails.

The business developer then devotes another 2 hours or more to writing the business development plans, remaining blog posts and any other progress reports required to give to the clients.

Then he can either stay back at the office and chat with the important people if any Business Development program is on the calendar or he can go back home to spend time with his family and loved ones.

By 9 PM, the Business Developer is ready to settle in for the night after some little catching up on the blogs and social media.

The next day would begin the same.

Therefore, we can conclude that the lifestyle of a Business Developer is quite a hectic one and keeps him on his toes for most part of the day; each day turns out to be more productive than another and each day brings new things to learn and know. Being a Business Developer is a commitment to hard work but isn't that a little price to pay for all the perks that Business Development as a career brings with itself.

HOW I GOT 100 MULTINATIONAL COMPANIES AS MY CLIENTS

Have a brilliant product but no one to buy it?

Okay imagine, you launched an amazing product or service, would it do any good without anyone buying it? Your product can't be sitting on the shelf and generating money! Someone must pay you in exchange for it.

Now, for instance you got your first customer or client; for how long will that sustain you? No matter how pricey your product or service might be, only one or a few clients don't really do the needed job, right? We are all here to make big cash in exchange of what we give.

Success for any business is defined by the continuous inflow of cash it has. If I were to get into the technical, when we forecast the present value of a business, we use the value of future cash flows to calculate it and cash flows is eventually how value is added and allotted to any business. This is a fact! Revenue and money is what we start business for! So, we need clients and we need a good number of clients, consistently buying our service. Am I right or am I right?

I can proudly say that I am a successful business developer and one of the major factors that I claim it to is being successful at being able to pitch a good number of clients!

As mentioned in the topic of the chapter, **I got hundred multinational companies from seven different countries as my clients.** I know it might sound a bit unbelievable but trust me, it is true! Yes! The number **100** is true! The number **7** is also true Just imagine the kind of revenue that I would have generated with 100 MNCs, not just singular clients or startups! It was not certainly but definitely preceded by a humongous amount of effort and initial work and learning; it also was a lot of work to manage this many big clients from across the world but I did it nonetheless. After all, what I had in my mind was the revenue I was going to garner ahead of the work I do; and I swear! It was huge!

Motivated enough? Pumped much? It is going to be huge for you too. Yes, it can be! If I can, why can you not? You can too. You will just need to put in hard work and smart work combined with efficient strategies, the right attitude and the mindset of a winner. You can do it too! And with me, you will!

In chapter 2, I walked you through my journey of getting that first client and a what a big shot it was! In this chapter I'll take you through the math that goes behind this.

I am a master Business Developer, right? Makes me great at marketing? Marketing is the be all and end all of any business. I have repeated this so many times already in this book so far. That is exactly what I did. Strategic marketing backed with the right business development plan helped me get these clients actually.

See, if ever you apply for a job, you're asked for a CV or an LOR, if you are in any event business you are asked for a portfolio, if you are in any service based business you're asked for testimonials, in a few other cases you might be asked for some sample work. Any which way, the client wants to know your record or your skills before putting the fate of their company in your hands. What can serve as a better testimonial than how you market and work on your own company first?

Your business is business development, how well you apply those skills to your own business eventually will determine how you will be able to attract and keep the clients. After all the best part you don't even need to pay a business developer to do that for you, you being there for it yourself and being the best at it, would you need anyone else? Showcase these amazing skills with the working of your own company and use them to pitch he clients.

There is no point in honing and learning these skills and sitting at home, waiting to use them to make money with your first client. This way you'll just keep sitting and dreaming and hoping only. This won't take you anywhere. Work smart and strategic. Use your skills to make your first client. Just like charity begins at home, Business Development begins at your own venture. You will eventually help build other people's business, why can't you first build your own?

Also, if we think of it this way, how well you market and work on your own business will send a fitting message to your prospective client on how well you'll do theirs.

I guess what I mentioned here was an obvious no brainer or was it not? Anyway any sensible person would do it but I just wanted to put this out there in my attempt to make this book a rather exhaustive source.

The best part about it all is that although you've to market and sell your business, as much as it sounds like a tedious task, the las thing you need to worry about is the fact that you'll need to go door to door to do so or have an actual functioning office with desks and cabinets to do so! That is the real beauty of the digital world, it is a kind of a work from home job! Where ever you may be, all you need to do is have a business and an efficient mindset to get that first client or even to be a successful business developer for that matter.

Once you start getting the clients, start claiming the authority when pitching the next client. Mention who it is that you work for, like I mentioned testimonials somewhere earlier in this chapter, it is bound to attract you more attention. That is the number one rule in pitching clients. Even if your first client wasn't a big shot, it doesn't matter. What matters is that you worked for someone and then how well you accomplished that work irrespective of the stature of your client. This is how you build your own brand and create your own market step by step. However, this all depends on first how you applied those skills to suit your needs and improve your business.

Secondly, put your best work forward to get a chance to put your best foot forward. I know this is backfilling bias and survivorship bias and what not, but eventually your best work is in the end your work only. You don't want to waste their time and your time I sending them a plethora of record when they're only interested in what value you can add to their company; just show them the value you had added to other companies. Why beat about the bush when you need to pluck just one rose? Makes sense?

Thirdly, who will your actual client be? People who are either starting off and have a lot of investment put at risk or people who are already doing well but want to take it to another level now because of either stagnation or coming up of competitors. They need people with a vision. Read through their business, read through their niche, read through their market; now since you're a master business developer you will automatically in the back of your head start coming up with solutions to their situation. This may come across as a bit strange but don't be afraid of pitching them by suggesting them an idea or two. Trust me this projection of suggestion will send a suggestibility of your interest in their business and will help cultivate the potential client's interest in working with you.

Fourthly, keep your pitch short, crisp, interesting and to the point. The potential client doesn't have time to go through an entire script, neither do you have the time to prepare an entire script. A very intelligent person might be able to write and write and write about a certain topic but the real efficiency is in explaining the same in a concise manner. Provide most value in as short a proposal as possible, keep it really simple. Nobody is paying you to prepare a quiz and no client is interested in deciphering a proposal that looks nothing less than a riddle. Don't be bogged down by the need to have a flowery proposal. You are not trying to pitch a writing contract, you are pitching a Business Development contract and that is what you need to know all about and that is what you need to focus on sharing and advertising about you. Keep it short and simple and you will without any doubt increase your probability of getting that client to a 100%.

Finally, Be very confident about your work. Know that you know all about it. Stop, listen to them and then answer accordingly. Don't be double dealing. They are investing in you as much as they are investing in the service that you have to offer.

You can do all of this all of this sitting at your home, even for an overseas client. That is exactly why and how amazing Business Development is! You can sit at one place and still have and work for clients all across the world.

All in all, what you are going to do is to get a contract from a client and then either giving the head start to their business or pulling them out of stagnation because 80-90% of businesses that begin, fail to sustain. Most of these businesses have a heavy seed investment behind them and are really desperate to have someone to handle their business for them. This is where you step in. You are the one who is going to use your skills to keep them going and going successful but first you need to have the skill to reach out to potential clients and convince them yourself. You need to sell your business first in order to find businesses to make sales for.

You convince them, get business from them, build their business, get more business. This forms a circle and a win-win situation for one and all. Just being a Business Developer doesn't serve the purpose, being a successful one does. You didn't spend all that time to learn those skills for nothing.

The one and only thing that I did to get myself a 100 clients from 7 different countries was the right kind of business strategy and the right kind of marketing. It also ensured bettering my skills because I was experimenting on myself observing the cause and effect from close.

To conclude, your first client is your own business which you have to subject to your effortless skills to get clients and then do the same for them. So, another beauty of Business Development is that you don't have to lose sleep about getting that first client because the first client is you. Be efficient with this first client and nothing will ever stop you from becoming a Business Development mogul!

ADVANTAGES OF HAVING A YOUTUBE CHANNEL

If a photo's worth a thousand words, then how much more valuable is video?

We've all grown up watching TV and reading books. Liars are they who would say they didn't enjoy watching TV more. Human minds are designed to connect better with a video, a 3d visual has a better, more engaging and more appealing effect on the person watching the videos than a blank canvas that a book offers you with.

Any person connects quicker and better with a video because a video has so many components that make it more engaging. The 3D visuals, the moving film, the audio and the graphics. The content from the video percolates better into mind than the written content because videos are one of the most self-explanatory tools out there.

Do you remember the smart classes in school? Weren't you able to grasp the lesson better via those video classes?

Okay so if you want to look up for a recipe; you can buy a book, google it or look up for it on YouTube and we all know you'll gain the best value in shortest possible time from YouTube.

If you want to look up for a review, you're more likely to watch one on YouTube and derive better information from there.

All in all, videos are a better mode of content communication, more impactful, more appealing and more attractive.

Coming back to YouTube, there are uncountable number of YouTube channels delivering a wide variety of content. No wonder, becoming a youtuber is one of the most attractive career options that people these days seemingly pursue. It gets you both money and fame. Little girls are making themselves a fortune recording themselves doing their makeup, little guys are making millions teaching video game tricks. Youtube is already the big thing and it is only bound to get bigger and better with time.

This brings us to another concept that is quite popular within te Business Development community, which is Video Marketing.

VIDEO MARKETING

In a nutshell, the concept of video marketing is the marketing of your product or service using videos as a medium to reach as many people as you can.

Video marketing can be used for everything from building customer rapport, to promoting your brand, services or products. Additionally, video marketing can serve as a medium to present how-to's, promote customer testimonials, live-stream events and deliver viral content .to make the potential clients more curious yet better acquainted with your services. It is a forward facing strategy that integrates engaging videos into your marketing campaigns.

STRATEGIES FOR VIDEO MARKETING

Right Resources

To create really appealing videos, you might need to invest in a good quality camera and editing tools. But quality sells and in the end, it's an investment, will last long and will give multiplied returns in the long run.

Tell Your Story, Don't Intend To Make A Sale

There is a heap of sales clutter on the Internet that is actively annoying and repelling your customers. Everything we do has a story behind it, and even if there isn't one, it doesn't harm to create one. Storytelling is what makes sales and that is what you are trying to do with the video so figure out the why and the how and put your brain to some solid workout. However, you don't want to throw your product in their face. Don't let your brand be that guy – instead, your video should be centred around the story and not the sale. concentrate on the value you're providing for your customers.

Make the most of the emotive power of video by appealing to your consumers' needs and hidden desires.

Engaging Content

Your content must be hooking and I cannot stress enough upon the importance of it. No one wants to spend their time streaming to listen to a boring piece of content so make sure your story has substance and is disseminated in an appealing manner. The takeaway here is to not feel constrained by what's gone before in your industry and don't try to emulate your competitor's stiff tone and yawn some script. Stand out and take a chance on being funny.

Keep It Short

Didn't I mention in the previous chapter as well that beating about the bush does no good to anyone? Get right to the grit of the tale and manage expectations from the outset within the first 5 to 10 seconds; else people will click out of the video in search of another.

Try sparking your audience's curiosity by asking questions and using teasers to hook their attention right away.

Your video should immediately convey its value and answer that "why should I watch it?" question that will be on your audience's mind. Should they watch it because it will make them laugh, because it will inspire them to act or because it will teach them something new?

Cut through the irrelevant stuff, get to the point like a master story teller and that is your perfect video marketing right there.

Educate Your Customers With Video

Your audience is a visual learner. One of the most powerful methods you can use for video marketing is to educate your audience. And the great thing is that education comes in many forms.

For example, you can teach your customers how to use your product or service and provide useful tips on how to make the most of it. Or you can create a video to showcase your industry knowledge, position your brand, add value to your consumers' lives and collect leads in the process by linking your website in the video description.

Video can also provide social proof for your product or service. When creating video success stories focus on the story of your customer and the success he achieved from using your product or service. These could serve as the testimonials much needed when pitching clients.

BENEFITS OF VIDEO MARKETING

Video helps you **connect with your audience**. Today, so much of a company's marketing efforts are designed to build trust. Video is the bridge that links what you say to who you really are, allowing customers to know your brand.

Video is an SEO gold mine, and helps to build backlinks to your site, boosting likes and shares which affects search rankings, and drives traffic to your site. And since YouTube is owned by Google, so be sure to post your videos with keywords!

Videos **boost information retention.** If your customers hear something only, they're likely to retain about 10% of that information three days later; by contrast, if what they hear is accompanied by relevant imagery, they'll retain an average 65% of that information three days later. This is a fact.

A good video marketing can attract new visitors.

Email subject lines that include the word "video" see a **20% increase in open rates,** and a **65% boost in click-throughs.**

Most of your potential customers would **prefer to watch a product video,** than read a product description because videos are quicker to watch and easier to understand.

You are here to sell, hence do consider that after watching a video, customers are 65-85% more likely to make a purchase.

However, the video making needs to be strategic, How to build a solid and **effective video marketing strategy,** how to **create content that people want to consume,** and how to **create engaging videos that get shared.** Additionally, video content marketers need to have a solid understanding of metrics about their indicators of a video's success and areas for improvement.

A YOUTUBE CHANNEL

Coming back to what I introduced in the beginning of the chapter, the surge in the use of YouTube. As I mentioned there are countless number of YouTubers out there and most of them are promoting their business via their channels. So, we must make the most of this trend, must we not?

YouTube is that omnipotent force that can help take any business to the next level.

Tap Into The Horde of YouTube Traffic

Online video is growing exponentially, with **over 4 billion videos viewed daily.** If you use YouTube for your business, you can easily reach your audience, both by creating videos and advertising on other people's videos.

- YouTube is the 2nd largest search engine and the 3rd most visited website worldwide, behind only Google and Facebook respectively.
- 1 billion people visit YouTube each month globally
- 100 hours of video are uploaded every 60 seconds to YouTube
- YouTube reaches more adults aged than any cable network

Video-streaming platforms like YouTube have become so big you're guaranteed to find a group of people who will become your fans and customers, as long as you educate, entertain and provide solutions to their problems.

Marketing on YouTube Will Help You Get Found on Google

Due to Google Universal Search, videos, images, news, books and local searches are blended together in Google's search results, so as to provide the most useful information for people searching.

You might have noticed that videos on YouTube appear more often in Google's search results. This shows that Google considers video to be as important as other pages.

You can take advantage of this by writing high-quality articles on your site and creating complementary videos in YouTube. Doing this will build backlinks to your site, and you will get found on Google more often by people searching.

Your Content Never Dies

Using YouTube for business can help you to re-purpose content you've already created without the need to spend a lot of time or to invest in expensive equipment.

Re-purposing content you have already created is an effective form of content marketing, as you can reach an audience that will love a particular type of content.

Grow Your Audience Worldwide

This is one of the biggest benefits of using YouTube for business.

Consistently creating video content opens the door to new visitors who would never come across your business any other way. Through

YouTube, you can reach a worldwide audience even if you only speak one language.

Considering that English is the most common language across the globe, if you make videos in English you're at an advantage,

In addition to this, if you include closed-captions on your videos, you can also reach new audiences as you are catering to people with different needs.

Research has shown that videos with closed-captions receive 4% more views and subscribers than those without.

It's also crucial to include several call-to-actions inside your videos, with links to direct the viewers to:

- Other videos on your channel.
- Content on your website.
- Email auto-responder series.
- Products and services on offer.

Build Your Email List In YouTube

Another benefit of using YouTube for business is the ability to build your email list as you continue to provide valuable, engaging content.

Use software that allows you to embed your sign-up form directly into YouTube videos. A video can be stopped temporarily for a viewer to enter their email address and subscribe to your list, before they continue. For that, you can even promise to send them some valuable free content on their email once they enter their email addresses. You can later market your product using this E-mail list.

Using this approach makes it easier than ever to build your email list, whilst providing engaging video content your audience will love.

Your Audience Will Promote You and Be Your Customer Too:

Videos with a personal touch help to increase conversions. People buy from those they trust, and that trust is built by you relating to them on an emotional level.

If you appear on your videos, they know who the person involved is and as a result, they tend to trust you more.

Research now shows that, for professional services and general companies, if you are driving traffic to a landing page with a video of a person in the company speaking about the product or service, it can dramatically increase your list of leads and sales.

Target Your Audience with AdWords for Video

With Google AdWords for Video, you can get laser-focused access to your audience by advertising on videos your audience are more likely to watch and search for.

The biggest advantage of AdWords for Video is that you'll only pay for engaged views.

An engaged view occurs when a viewer watches your ad for at least 30 seconds. If your video ad is skipped by the viewer, you won't pay anything.

The biggest benefit of AdWords for Video is the potential to grow your audience through 'earned views' which is organic.

AdSense For The Video

Creating regular video content gives you the opportunity to earn some money directly from your videos, through Google's AdSense for Video program

You can use Google AdWords and AdSense for Video together to make some money back from your video campaigns too.

If the Viewer sees your video ad in another video and clicks on it, you pay for that click as part of your campaign budget.

Then the viewer proceeds to watch your video, viewing the ads from other content creators that are enabled to display on your videos

The viewer then clicks or watches those ads and you are paid 68% of the ad revenue.

This means that you can run AdWords campaigns for your videos, whilst making money by allowing others to advertise on your videos.

As you can see YouTube is a viable platform for making money, growing your audience and business in a number of ways.

If you invest the required time to learn the main components of the platform, YouTube will show itself to be a worthwhile addition to grow your bank balance as well as to promote your business.

HOW TO USE YOUTUBE TO YOUR ADVANTAGE

1. **Get other website owners to embed your videos on their websites**

   When someone else embeds your video in their website, it counts as a vote in the favor of your video. The more the number of people who embed your video, the higher it will rank in the search results, as Google gives a priority to websites that have great content, which is updated regularly.

2. **Associate your domain name with your YouTube channel**

   Associating your website with your channel will reflect that you are the official representation of your company or brand on YouTube. This will result in more relevant video results pointing to your business when someone searches for your brand or terms that are similar to the services you offer.

3. **Get your videos shared on social media platforms**

   Social media metrics are a factor taken into consideration when ranking pages on the Google search engine page results. If you can create high-quality videos that entices others to share, you're signaling to Google that you are producing content that is valuable to your target audience and its algorithm will start pushing you higher on the search results page.

4. **Give your audience more options to consume**

   Providing your audience with a variety of ways to consume information – including text, video illustrations and audios – will increase the overall engagement your videos receive, as you are catering to different learning styles and taking away the monotony of the learning process.

   This all is an exhaustive idea of the wonders that YouTube can do to your business. So now you know that a YouTube channel is not to be left out at any cost.

COLD CALLING: HOW & WHY

Across the business market, there float various misconceptions about what cold calling is. No! No! You're not picking your phone and dialing random number and trying to sell yourself! You're not a crazy stalker or teaser. This is a very misconstrued portrayal of what cold calling actually is.

Cold calling is the solicitation of a potential customer who had no prior interaction with a business person looking for customers. A form of telemarketing, cold calling is one of the oldest and most common forms of marketing for businessmen. It is a technique in which a salesperson contacts individuals who have not previously expressed interest in the offered products or services. Cold calling typically refers to solicitation by phone or telemarketing.

There are a few other types of marketing techniques under the header of "calling", which business developers must be aware of and let us now delve into them and learn how they are different from cold calling.

WARM CALLING

Warm Calling refers to contacting the prospect clients with whom you've had prior contact. The stronger the contact between you and the prospect, the more effective the warm call is going to be.

For example, if you had met a prospect at some industry event or business event and if he asks you to give him a call so that you can set up an appointment, that would be an **extremely warm call**. On the other hand, if you send a letter or an email to a prospect and then follow up with a phone call, that would be more of **a lukewarm call**.

A prospect who's been referred to you also qualifies as a warm call, even though you haven't directly been in contact with that prospect. The fact that the referrer is recommending you to the prospect creates a connection, even if indirect, between you and the prospect. The prospect may not know you, but he knows the person who referred you to him, so the referrer is a sort of bridge and a middleman making the call still kind of warm.

Another type of warm call occurs when a prospect has reached out to you for more information. For example, a prospect might have filled out a form on your website where they visited to learn about the industry you work in requesting a callback or call a general number in response to an ad they had come across somewhere. These prospects are usually intrigued enough to go to the effort of reaching out to you, but they don't actually know anything about you personally. These warm leads are certainly easier to work with, but will still need some rapport building on your front.

Truly warm calls are much easier to convert to appointments because the prior contact or connection with the prospect establishes that you already have a bit of trust between you. Hence, the prospect will be more willing to invest time in hearing what you have to say and will also be more invested in the conversation. Many salespeople make it a goal to do only warm calling, since not only are warm calls more productive, they're also less likely to result in rejection, which makes them far more pleasant to the salesperson's as an experience.

Dividing up your calls into cold calls and warm calls can be tricky because the classification is based off of your point of view, not of the prospect's point of view. If you've been in contact with the prospect before but he doesn't even remember speaking with you, then from his point of view it's a cold call but you yourself would classify it as a warm call. This is a confusing mix of things.

If you are in any doubt as to how the prospect views you, it's best to treat the call as though it is a cold call. Assuming that you have a relationship with the prospect when you actually don't will only annoy him and make it harder for you to get that appointment because that'll make you come across as some cocky and clingy person.

However, whilst the chances of converting the call are better, that does not imply that you try to make a sale during the call. Selling should take place during your appointment, not in a brief phone call. The exception is inside salespeople who are to make sales only over the phone. For everyone else, it is kind of imperative that selling should take place either during a real or a virtual meeting.

When making a warm call, first introduce yourself and then soon bring up your pre-existing connection with the prospect. Again, do not beat about the bush! His response will do much to tell you whether this is actually a warm call after all. If he says he doesn't remember you or otherwise responds unenthusiastically, shift the approach and treat him as a cold lead. If he does acknowledge the connection, you can move forward with confidence and treat the call as warm.

SOCIAL CALLING

Social selling is exactly what it sounds like: using social media to essentially sell a service, good or product. But unlike the typical sales call or direct marketing campaign, for instance, the act of social selling is more of a lead generating activity, and therefore it sits at the top of the sales funnel.

However, the term social selling can be a little bit misleading in that it's not really about 'the sale'; it's about prospecting, engagement, and relationship-building. It's also a very useful tool when it comes to informing, educating, and building brand awareness.

Around 70% of a buyer's journey takes place in the digital space, and most of the time in this digital era, people conduct an online research before making a purchasing decision.

This means that the information they're seeing about products and services in their social feeds is bound to make an impact and, there's plenty of reason for people to be choosy and careful about who they're partnering with.

Social selling is also useful for connecting with others, especially influencers in their field such as thought leaders or celebrities. When you're networking, you're usually looking to follow others with a strong social media following and influence so that you can essentially sell products off of their audience.

The reason why social selling works is that it's offering us a new way to have real, two-way conversations. As consumers and clients, we don't need to listen to a 'pitch' when we have more and more information available to choose what we purchase and who we partner with.

To put it in simpler words: social selling is more meaningful even though it may not convert directly, it's probably just going to feel more like an equal exchange and less like a one-way conversation.

The concept behind social selling is that it allows your prospect to engage with you in a low-pressure way – that is, by choice. However, using social selling can be more effective because:

- It gives the receiver the option of responding when they have the time
- It allows the receiver to gather information about a product or service so that they can make a choice as to whether or not they want to have a conversation about it
- It relieves the emotional pressure on both ends of the conversation.

When you are engaging with people in your field, especially leaders who you learn from, you're doing some form of social selling. And connecting with them need not be daunting or complex. There are plenty of tools out there to help you understand who you want to connect with as well as how you connect with them.

So long as you understand what you're offering, you can use any social media platform to connect with people in your industry , LinkedIn in this case will be the best option, simply because it does have a decidedly professional focus.

If you are innovative about using the tools provided on the site, you can find people easily – for instance, by asking for referrals from existing contacts.

There are a number of tools that you can use either within LinkedIn or in conjunction with it that can do a lot of the drudgery for you – research that in the past would have been quite time-consuming to do.

For instance, the tool **Crystal** gives you information and insights into people's work styles and personality types in order to guide you towards the best ways of connecting with them. And tools like **SalesLoft** Prospector gather data for you across multiple channels in order to offer real-time information about various companies and contacts which them you can use as you deem fit to make a call to them.

Even if you're just sticking to LinkedIn for your networking, even that provides you with a plenty of opportunities to boost your authority and visibility via simple blog posts and Slide share slideshows.

Another area that social selling is useful for is personal branding by combining both personal and professional presence and the transperancy that you create will make people trust what you're doing and what you have to say.

COLD CALLING

Coming back to cold calling as the master step in pitching clients; people think that with the existence of warm and social calling; cold calling no more holds the relevance it did. However, it is not true. Cold calling very much still works brilliantly if done the right way. As mentioned before, Cold calling is in plain terms contacting any prospect who currently isn't "raising their hand" at the moment.

So even if you call your best client and ask for referrals, when you call that referral, it's still a "cold call" because the prospect didn't ask to be contacted nor was expecting your call. But, that's OK! A salesperson shouldn't base the prospects on what the 'temperature' of the call is, how much they know about the prospect but rather on how much the prospect knows and has an interest in the product or service a salesperson is selling.

Ideally, your phone would be ringing off the hook all day with clients offering you business but the reality is that it is you wants business so it is you that needs to go after it, and as part of your outbound marketing strategy, cold calling can be a very effective sales tactic if it›s done properly.

According to a recent survey by DiscoverOrg, 60% of more than 1,000 polled senior executives from the IT industry reported taking an appointment or attending an event after receiving a cold call or unsolicited email. So, the bottom line is that, IT WORKS!

WHY IS COLD CALLING IMPORTANT?

Cold calling has a very specifically defined purpose which is to have a human-to-human interaction with your prospects. Often, this purpose is forgotten not because it's not important, but because most sales people feel uncomfortable doing it.

As a matter of fact, telemarketing and cold calling remains an important discipline to have before applying to any sales role. Prospecting via phone calls remains a great complement to your overall appointment setting and lead generation activities.

With all of this being said, the importance of cold calling boils down to this: **it's a cost and time efficient method of targeted, human-to-human lead generation.**

When you can clearly define and identify who your prospects are, cold call telemarketing is a great way to hustle for new business opportunities and clients. It becomes even more effective when advertising and marketing budgets, limit or prohibit other forms of lead generation because cold calling is extremely cost-effective.

Cold calling remains an efficient lead generation method, giving you control over growing your business, while not depending upon inbound generation methods.

HOW TO SUCCESSFULLY COLD CALL?

1. **Focus on the goal**

   Beginners tend to think that cold calling is about making the sale. It's not. It's about getting the chance to make the sale. Specifically, the purpose of a cold call is to set an appointment to make the pitch which is why it is so important that you should not make a sale on a cold call.

2. **Research your markets and prospects thoroughly before jumping into cold calling them**

   You need to target your cold calling to the right audience. Use market research to focus on your target market. Then find out as much as you possibly can about the company or individual you're going to call in advance. This gives you the huge advantage of being able to talk about their business and their needs when you call them, which will show that you are actually interested in working with them.

   Also, connecting with the right people is critical to your cold calling success.

3. **Improve your chances to connect by leveraging the social media contacts**

   According to a research, if the person you are calling is in a common LinkedIn group you are 70% more likely to get to speak with them on a cold call. And what's true of LinkedIn is true of other social media platforms as well; having a connection through a social media group will increase the prospect's receptiveness when you reach out to contact them which gives you all the more reason to work on improving your social media presence.

4. **Prepare an opening statement for your call**

   This lets you organize your thoughts before calling, and helps you avoid common mistakes in the opening that would give the person you're calling the chance to terminate the conversation. You definitely don't want to sound random and if you go unprepared, out of nervousness, you wouldn't be able to carry the conversation forward. Prepare for getting the conversation off to a good start.

5. **How to frame the cold call's opening statement?**

   Include a greeting and an introduction, a reference point, the benefits of your product or service, and a transition to a question or dialogue and keep all of it as concise and precise as possible.

6. **Frame the rest of your cold call as well**

   Lay out the benefits of your product or service and the reasons your prospect should buy. Write out possible queries they may put and your answer to them. Without a cold calling script, it's too easy to leave something out or talk irrelevant. Once again, it's not that you'll be reading your script word for word when you call and sound like a 10 year old narrator to a play, but that you've prepared the framework of the cold call in advance

   Also prepare yourself to answer detailed questions about your products and services! You won't be sending out a good message if you are unable to answer about the service that you called to offer.

7. **Be specific about the appointment date and time during your cold call**

   "Would Friday at 10 a.m. be a good time to meet?" is a better way to propose to fix an appointment than saying "Can I meet with you to discuss this next week?" You want to get your prospect to commit to a meeting during this first call rather than leaving it vague which will call the need for a second call to set up a meeting - which may never happen if you can't get through with the call to the prospect again.

8. **Smooth the way for your call by sending prospects a small, unique promotional item**

   This helps break the ice and makes your business stand out from the crowd. During the call, when you mention your name, they might remember that you sent them a present. This might sound a bit phony but it really helps in carrying the conversation further.

9. **Do your cold calling early in the morning or late in the afternoon**

   These are the best times to reach the decision-maker directly. Research upon the best days for making the cold call too. Once, these external favors are in your favor and you are well prepared with the call, you increase your probability of getting success from the call.

10. **Persist**

    Research says that 80% of new sales are made after the fifth contact, yet the majority of salespeople give up after the second call, out of fear, embarrassment or irritation. Don't be one of those who gives up so easily. If you want to make the sale, you need to try and try again. Remember, it is you who needs to get business so it is you who has to do the chasing.

11. **Practice**

    Practice brews perfection. So, practice, practice, practice. While cold calling may never be much fun for you, you can get better at it, and the more you practice, the more effective your call will be. So get your script and your call list together and reach for the phone. The people who want to do business with you or buy your product are out there but how will they do it if they do not know about you. Take the reins them know about you first.

PERSONAL BRANDING

Steve Jobs used personal branding well before the phrase was even well known to distinguish himself as the face of Apple. Elon Musk's personal brand is probably better known than Tesla's corporate brand. It makes sense that any business owner or manager should bond with potential customers first on an individual basis before he or she tries to deliver the company's message.

The idea of "personal branding" is unusual to most people. But it is very important to know that in this online era, where things; both good and bad, last forever on the internet, personal branding can be considered more important than ever.

Personal Branding is how you promote yourself. It is the unique combination of skills, experience, and personality that you want the world to see about you. It is the telling of your story yourself, and how it reflects your conduct, your behavior. Personal branding is a process wherein you take conscious and intentional effort to create a perception and influence of yourself by positioning yourself as an authority and establishing credibility of yourself. All of this is to communicate and present your value to the world in order to root yourself as a respectable brand in the heads of the people.

You use your personal branding to differentiate yourself from other people. Done well, you can tie your personal branding in with your business in ways no corporate branding can possibly succeed.

Professionally, your personal brand is the image that people see of you. It can be a combination of how they look at you in real life, how the media portrays you, and the impression that people gain from the information about you available online.

You can either ignore your personal brand, and let it develop organically, possibly chaotically, beyond your control, or you can help establish your personal brand your way via customized process of personal branding to depict you as the person you want to be depicted as.

Your personal brand can be vital to you professionally. It is how you present yourself to current and potential clients. It gives you the opportunity to ensure that people see you in the way you want them to, instead of in some arbitrary, possibly detrimental way.

It gives you the opportunity to highlight your strengths and your passions. It helps people believe they know you better, and people have much higher trust in those they feel they know; even pubic people they have never met personally.

The impact of personal branding can be seen very prominently at the time of elections. Most people vote for the name they recognize instead of voting for the promises that a person is making. Is it a surprise to you that people with strong personal brands succeed better at politics?

Personal branding is of utmost necessity when it comes down to creating an influence on people because influence is what is going to make people buy into you and buy into your business. If you are branded a con man, only a fool would invest with you. If you are branded the mogul in that industry, only a fool wouldn't invest with you. Any which way, the only medium that people know you through is the image and reputation that you have made for yourself and the story of yourself that you have chosen to narrate to the world. And what they know about you is what you tell them about yourself.

The stronger your personal branding is, the stronger your influence will be. It is eventually your personal brand that makes you unique and memorable and makes you stand out from the crowd.

Okay, so for instance, a consumer happens to see an advertisement, there is some probability that they might click on that ad, then there is also some probability that they consider buying the product but this probability is bound to rise exponentially if the person behind the advertisement has a strong personal brand and an even greater influence. People will have faith in a person with a stronger personal brand and would not think much before becoming a customer to that service.

This, and I cannot stress upon this enough, is the reason why influential marketing is becoming so successful. Have you seen your favorite influencer endorsing a product more than you see an advertisement of that product here and there? Well the product is still being advertised, just not from behind the curtains but by someone who has created a massive following behind them and earned trust of their followers. In this case, the companies are leveraging on the personal branding of these influencers.

It is more of an emotional connection and is not as easy as it comes across as. This is because anyone can take fancy pictures and write flowery captions to lure people but it takes time to hone in on your authentic message and build a true brand that is deep rooted and bound to work no matter what.

Unfortunately, a lot of people get uncomfortable about the concept of personal branding, some people even dismiss the process as being too time consuming, or not that important; but if you don't build it, you'll be missing out on a lot of opportunities because people tend to put their faith in places where they know the person involved as well as they would have known them personally.

WHAT MAKES PERSONAL BRANDING INEVITABLY IMPORTANT?

People are tracking you at every stage of your career

Regardless of your age or professional stage, someone is screening you online. What they find can have major implications for your professional and personal well-being. Keeping a track of your social media activity is the closest such people can get to know how you brand yourself. If you aren't properly managing your online reputation, you're missing out on a lot of business.

This might not matter much for people with jobs, but for freelancers and entrepreneurs, a personal brand is something which can make or break them.

For big enterprises, around 40% of the company's reputation is attributed to the reputation of the CEO.

Personal Branding guides you on your next step

The most important reason to focus on personal branding is to help yourself.

Personal branding is a painless but extremely necessary step in working towards your goals. Regardless of your industry or professional status, your personal brand has the power to make or break all kinds of opportunities for advancement.

When building your brand starts to feel like a job, remember that it is an essential part of cultivating your career and that the greatest investment of resources, time and effort will likely come up front.

Building and optimizing new profiles, generating content about you and your work, identifying your goals, building a brand strategy - this can certainly feel overwhelming. But once you've established a strong foundation, you'll have a roadmap to follow, which makes the whole process pretty manageable.

THE HOW OF BUILDING A PERSONAL BRAND

Building a personal brand is not a one-time or an overnight job, it is an ongoing process and must be divided into smaller achievable and probable phases.

PHASE 1: BASICS- LOOK THE PART

First of all, you will need to scrutinize and customize your search results and clean up the content that doesn't align what you want to serve to the world. Get rid of anything you don't envision as a part of your personal brand. Mostly, stuff that projects unprofessional behavior includes unprofessional communication style, drinking or drug abuse, criminal behavior, polarizing views, sexually explicit content and bigotry.

PHASE 2: TELL THEM ABOUT YOURSELF

Identify everything that makes you unique and makes you stand out from the crowd. Now present it to your audience in a very transparent and personal manner addressing who you are, what your goals are, what your skills are; and do it all with evidence to make it more authentic and see your sales shoot like anything.

PHASE 3: WHY SHOULD THEY CHOOSE YOU?

There could be a plethora of people offering the same service as yours then why should a person choose your service and not theirs. Well, you need to tell them about your skills, about your X factor, about your persistence and commitment. There should be a solid reason for anyone to choose you and for that you need to remove competition by just showing why you could be a better and more viable choice.

PHASE 4: BUILD AN ONLINE PRESENCE TO REFLECT YOU AND YOUR EXPERTISE:

Now that you have all the content in place, it should be written properly, published at all write places and promoted efficiently. There are a LOT of social media websites that you can create profiles on; Instagram, Facebook, twitter, LinkedIn, Pinterest, medium, Tumblr, vimeo, YouTube; to name a few!

After you've created these profiles, optimize them for the search engine and thereafter you will need to constantly update and maintain the content to make it look more authentic.

BENEFITS OF PERSONAL BRANDING

YOU CAN BE YOURSELF

Personal branding teaches you that it is okay to be yourself, you do not have to live a life of pretense in order to impress people out there, you just need to grow as a person that you have always been and isn't that necessary too, to always keep growing as a better version of yourself. Moreover, as you will come out into the crowd as yourself and realize how much love and respect you garner in being that, your self-esteem will increase too.

BOOSTS YOUR CONFIDENCE

As you sit down to jot down your skills and achievements, you finally get to realize that you had been underestimating yourself all this time, that there is so much potential in you to succeed and be anything you want to be. This will make your confidence soar.

CREDIBILITY

If your words align with your actions and you live up to your personal brand, if you do what you told people you were going to do, you automatically build yourself as a credible person to do business with or buy services from.

WHY YOU?

Personal Branding is the smoothest way to showcase your specialty via displaying your experiences, your achievements and your skills. You can't be good at everything? So you need to specify your niche and speak about what is it that makes you unique in that niche and how is it that you claim your expertise in that niche.

CREATE A MARK

The purpose of personal branding is to have you leave a mark behind yourself; to make sure that people remember you by your skills, expertise, actions and the connection that you make. However, defining a personal brand implies that you need to be brave enough to let your true self be visible.

CONNECT TO THE AUDIENCE

Your audience is eventually where your clients will come from. You need to develop a strong connection with your audience by being more transparent which creates a sense that your audience knows you up close. This connection however will benefit more if customized according to your target audience. You can't be a tech company and try to benefit from connecting with fashion centered audience. Know your niche and accordingly target the audience. Then build a personal brand also accordingly to become more familiar with your target audience and hence more credible and hence garner more trust and hence more clients, probably long term ones!

LET YOURSELF BE

Even though building a personal brand is not a walk in the park, you do not have to reinvent yourself in anyway in order to hardwire your uniqueness into the minds of people. You just have to discover and re-discover yourself and once that is done, this ongoing process works for itself and for you as well.

You just need to do the hard work upfront and then be consistent about it.

INFLUENCER MARKETING

The hottest trend floating around social media right now is INFLUENCERS or BLOGGERS!

Their flashy lifestyle is making more and more people take up a career of becoming an influencer either as a full time career or as a side hustle.

What an influencer really is? An influencer, as the word suggests is someone who builds an audience, builds trust in them and then recommends products and services using their influence upon their audience.

Why has influencer marketing become so popular? Remember those times when your favorite celebrities used to promote the products? Why not anymore? As the trend of influencers started taking over, brands realized that the people in the marketplace put their trust in the influencers more than they put it in the celebrities. These influencers have established connection with their audience via personal branding and people are more likely to buy a product that an influencer recommends, instead of buying something that a celebrity recommends. Moreover, influencers are easier to access and more affordable too.

But, is that it? We live and breathe influencer marketing everyday yet we don't truly know what it is.

WHAT IS INFLUECER MARKETING?

It is a form of marketing which uses key influencer in a market to drive and spread the brand's message to a larger market. Rather than marketing yourself to the audience, you instead hire and pay an influencer who has better influence over the niche targeted audience to spread your message.

Influencer Marketing basically takes 2 forms: content marketing and social media marketing.

Most of the social media campaigns have a component in which the influencers are required to share the content that you give them or they are required to generate content themselves and then use it to spread the message of the brand across their social media channels. Since people put their faith in influencers, and view them as people who are just like themselves; the conversion rate is likely to be very high. This is how content is generated and shared across social media and this is how social media marketing and content marketing integrates into what we call influencer marketing.

If you use any kind of social media, which I am sure you do, I am guessing you already know as to how popular and effective it actually is.

WORD-OF-MOUTH MARKETING VERSUS INFLUENCER MARKETING

Both these methods of marketing are targeted at the traction of customers and deservedly so by building their trust in your brand through people whom they already trust. However, both methods are not the same.

Word-of-mouth marketing is any instance where consumers share information about a product or organization with one another, whether by talking or through some other medium. Internet communication, especially social networking, is a part of modern word-of-mouth marketing. The traditional method includes talking in person.

- In case of influencer marketing, there is usually as relationship between the influencer and the brand. This ensures some measure of accountability and reliability between both the parties because the influencer has a track record and hence a sense of obligation. Word-of-Mouth marketing on the other hand does not depend much on prior relationships. These are normal people sharing their reviews and recommendations to other strangers by communicating with them. Therefore, everyone is an influencer in some way.

- Since word-of-mouth marketing is more organic, authentic and ad-free; it doesn't guarantee the kind of marketing that is happening because no matter how good your product is, it might resonate more to some and less to the others. However, since influencer marketing is a paid promotion, there is more regulation as there is an obligation on the influencer now but it must be disclosed as an advertisement.

- Word-of-mouth marketing is usually more natural because the sharers are picking up the story and the reviews they want to sharer by themselves and are not paid to do so. In influencer marketing, the brand is basically borrowing the audience of the influencer with an engaged following to sell their product. The influencer is paid something by the brand for leveraging their hard earned audience and trust.

Reading through these, you might feel like there is an authenticity gap between both the methods of marketing. However, the gap is blurring out now. Influencers, even though they are paid to promote the product are still considered as trustable and authentic sources of information. A paid relationship with a big and lovable brand adds to the authenticity of the influencer.

ADVOCATE MARKETING VERSUS INFLUENCER MARKETING

Advocate Marketing means that a loyal customer is advocating your product and giving positive reviews to people about your brand. Such a customer must have been using your product for some time and is a more reliable reviewer for the people around. Advocate marketing focuses on incentivizing the loyal customers and encouraging them to share their love for you and your brand to more people.

Influencer marketing requires the brands to look for influencers and crack a deal with them and paying them either with money or free products. Advocate marketing focuses less on payment and more on driving brand loyalty.

IMPORTANCE OF INFLUENCER MARKETING

The economy of influence has changed the way we buy things. The way influencer marketing has become popular is because of how effective it actually is. It has more potential than people realize. Even people with a smaller following on social media can work as micro influencers and market the products to people who are visiting their page. With demand on the rise, the economy of influence is changing the buying behavior of customers. Brands who aren't catching up are losing their hold over the market because we need to adapt with changing times and if we don't we get left behind in the race.

Conventional Digital Marketing no longer works like it did before. Don't you get irritated by the repetitive ads that pop up in your feed?

Influencer marketing purges this "ad fatigue" as it delivers authenticity and there are no annoying repetitive ads or cookies popping up on your feed continually. Influencer marketing goes beyond clicks and reach and is more focused on continuous engagement to drive traffic and align with the objectives of your business that is to attract new customers, establish customer loyalty, create repeated purchases and maximizing revenue.

Customers are not lured by faceless executives anymore; they are more influenced by the influencers they see on screen because they know that now there is a real person involved. Customers can't ignore the influencers anymore and this is why content creators have a power to drive the business towards growth and engage audience through authenticity. That is the power of influencer marketing.

HOW DOES INFLUENCER MARKETING WORK?

Now that we have discussed how important influencer marketing is, we should also know how it actually works.

The landscape of marketing has changed significantly and consumers determine the content they want to see. If brands want to be a part of consumer conversations, they have to play by their rules. Social media is where consumers are having conversations today, and one of the most impactful methodologies is of influencer marketing. So how does influencer marketing work?

At a grassroots level, it is a form of engagement where brands leverage on those who boast prominent social footprints. The goal is to plug into new communities and connect the brand to new audiences through the voice and trusted relationships of influencer because their audience trusts in them.

Authentic content creates trust. People gravitate towards bloggers and influencers because they value the content that they create. Developing strategic relationships with these influencers allows brands to collaborate and create content and share it with consumers through a trusted source. To make the most of this opportunity, brands must allow influencers the ability to stay true to themselves even when working on sponsored content. Insincere content or content that pushes sales too much will rapidly erode an influencer's power by reducing their followers' trust in them to the detriment of one and all.

If brands want to be relevant to consumers, they must approach influencers as a way to attract, engage, and convert prospects. That means serving to the consumers with content they care about and trust. Working with influencers is an effective way to fuel a conversation about a brand using authentic content. Since influencer marketing results in engagement, it also results in conversions. Influencers are experts at generating discussions online, so the content they create on behalf of a brand is talked about, shared, and reposted. That is earned media. The earned media is trusted more by consumers.

Online activity is a core part of the decision making process. In today's digital world, people can access information about products long before they reach a brand site and this is what they actually do. Customers look for reviews online before they make a decision to buy a product. Therefore, it makes sense for brands to partner with social media influencers because they can provide these reviews to the customers. They have the ability to share product and brand information that shapes purchase decisions.

Social media has changed the way brands interact with consumers by creating an environment where consumers have immediate access to information. Through the influencers, people gather input about brands and products and then make purchase decisions based on what they discover. Successful brands leverage influencers to stay connected with consumers by actively participating in their decision making via the content being shared with them. However, traditional advertising is not the same as influencer marketing which means being part of the conversation. Working with influencers allows brands to add to the conversation rather than derailing it with is very likely to happen with traditional marketing.

Every brand must start using influencer marketing to their advantage and realize its infinite potential.

GETTING THE RIGHT MENTORS

Have you ever had bad experience with teachers at school? Experiences like they don't know what they are teaching, or they are very strict, or that they drag the topic too much or that they are just nor interesting or that they are very lenient?

School education is the building blocks of a child's life. What kind of teacher he has becomes utterly important in determining to some extent how effective the learning process is going to be. What is more important than the brand of the school the kid is being sent to is the quality of education that is being delivered which is in direct relation with the teachers that are appointed in the school.

If the teacher doesn't know, how will the student know? If the teacher knows but doesn't tell, how will the student know?

One can never overlook how important it is to have the right mentor in your journey to learn anything at any point in life. Sure thing, experiences teach better, self-education surpasses anything else; it will only benefit to have a mentor who can guide you in the right direction or guide you through as you pick a direction for yourself.

Mentoring is important, not only from the point of view of the knowledge and skills that an individual can learn but also because mentoring provides professional specialization and the right kind of support to facilitate the learning experience and outcome in any walk of life.

A three-quarter of executives express how critical the presence of mentor has been in shaping their career in the right way. Do you really have the time to shoot arrows in random directions before you can find where it is that your target is? It would certainly be helpful to drive away the randomness and work with focus in the direction of your destination. A well learned and experienced mentor can certainly do that task for you or at least help you out with it.

This is a fast paced era, as much as self-education will help you learn more, you don't want to learn more but rather learn what is necessary and having the right mentor is where the solution to it lies.

You, as a mentee, can derive immense value from the experiences of those that you view as your mentor. You need to find the right kind of mentor from whose personal investment in you, you can tap into your full potential and not let any of it go to waste.

The value of having a mentor whose journey complements yours can't be matched with anything else in the world. A deep professional relationship with a mentor like this can be a very gratifying experience to have.

As a child, your parents are your mentors and it reflects in your behavior throughout your life. Similarly, the way you carry on with your career and conduct yourself throughout the journey speaks volumes about who you've been mentored by.

As a person who is looking to earn financial freedom, either as an entrepreneur or a freelancer; you might feel like it would be exciting to embark on the journey alone as it would be an enlightening experience. However, even if you have a great idea but do not know how and where to begin or how and when to take it to next level; using help of a mentor can reduce the anxiety and help you achieve the much needed ad much deserved success.

FINDING THE MENTOR

Finding the right mentor whose journey complements yours or who you resonate with is as extremely critical because this person is going to guide you through your journey to success.

This process is supposed to be both organic and deliberate. Do not wait for a potential mentor to approach you. You need to put your foot forward and start finding opportunities to find the right mentor; connect with a manager, a colleague or a person whom you know to exhibit the values and practices you deem fit with your model. Sometimes you may want to look for more than one mentor if you are looking to advance yourself in a diverse number of functional skills at different phases of your career development or for different segments of the single stage in your career development. Your mission of finding a mentor can take place in any environment; your college, previous work place, current work place, social media, your previous business contacts or someone you heard about from a third party and are now looking to contact. Anyway, it is but important to remember that viable mentors are successful, experienced and busy people. Many possible mentor candidates are enthusiastic to bring on mentees, guide them, teach them, help them and create protégés, but they need to believe you truly want to succeed. Why would they invest themselves personally into a person who assumes it all to be a cake walk and treats it like a casual thing. They would rather put their time in someone else who would earn laurels for themselves as well as the mentor, who wouldn't let their hard work go to waste.

They need to believe from the beginning you are going to struggle through the hardships and take advice with an open heart and a willingness to execute with grit. It is very important when working with a mentor to also keep your attitude in check. It is okay to propose a suggestion but it is never okay to look for an argument. After all you are the one who has to learn and to learn you need to be humble and know that there is a scope for improvement.

To find the right mentor, first you need to become the right mentee. You must know your goals and objectives earlier on so that you can know what mentor might rightly fit your needs.

Ask yourself a few questions about your strengths, your weaknesses, skills that you want to learn, your goals, how dedicated you are, your learning style and if you are at the starting point or in the middle of your career. Once you find answers to these questions, it will be easier for you to analyze and look for a mentor that will be right for you and that you will be right for.

It is necessary to know the answers to these questions because this is where your process of recruiting the mentor that fit your needs, your style, your work-life balance and your missions begins.

There is another important question that goes into the process of finding the right mentor, that is, what are the skills that you already possess. This is because this is how you will be noticed by your potential investors. I know, it is said that a person who knows too much can't be taught well because a lot of unlearning needs to be done. However, with people like mentors who are bound to be super busy in their lives, it will be a daunting ask to really start from the basics and it would really help to teach someone who knows at least something about what he is about to learn.

If you are able to display your skills and impress an elusive mentor, you have hit the jackpot, so being aware of the initial skills you possess will only help you in getting that mentor that is perfect for you.

This way, you will also have established confidence within you that you are a smart and efficient learner and it will make the learning process both exciting and easier or both the mentor and the mentee.

However, when it comes back to where to fetch the mentor from, don't give up too soon, you need to persist in whatever you do in your life. Same is true when looking for a mentor. Go to conferences, cold call people, send mails, send LinkedIn invitations and continuously be there. Be proactive in finding a mentor irrespective of the industry or profession that you are in. Mentors don't seek you but you need to get noticed.

QUALITIES THAT YOU AS A POTENTIAL MENTEE MUST HAVE

Possesses intellectual curiosity and must know how to ask smart questions, must know where to put more energy to and where to put less energy to.

- Is receptive to guidance and open to learning just like I mentioned earlier in this chapter. A mentee must have a mindset of a learner, not that of a know it all. He must listen with intention and mutual respect and be very open to accepting difference in opinions and not turning them into baseless and open ended arguments.
- Highly engaged and hard working with whatever tasks are assigned. A devoted mentee will not run away from his duties towards his mentor and towards himself.
- Therefore, be what you are looking for. By saying this, I mean be the perfect mentee in your quest for a perfect mentor.

AN EXHAUSTIVE LIST OF WHY HAVING A MENTOR IS INDISPENSIBLE

1. **Mentors provide information and knowledge**

    As Benjamin Franklin said, "Tell me and I forget, teach me and I may remember, involve me and I learn." When starting out, you might have little or no idea what is involved in running a business, including making a business plan, budgeting, handling daily operations, making strategic decisions or running a marketing campaign. With a mentor there from the start, you can tap into the plethora and wealth of knowledge and take the reins of your career and that will get you to speed faster and shorten that learning curve.

2. **Mentors can see where we need to improve where we often cannot**

   There is a reason why they are mentors. They can see that about you which you cannot and this approach that mentors have is what actually helps you grow. They will always be brutally honest with you and tell you exactly how it is rather than downplay any weaknesses they see in you.

   This constructive criticism that mentors offer help you to see things in yourself that you might not recognize, provided you do not take the criticism upon your ego and take it as constructive. Take it as an opportunity to learn from their experiences and use them to grow out of your weaknesses.

3. **Mentors find ways to stimulate our personal and professional growth**

   Your mentor learns a lot about you in the process of working together. Your mentor will assign you tasks which if you see through completion will help you grow personally and professionally. He will then tell you what he observed about you throughout the process and which qualities he deems fit to be kept intact and which to be reprogrammed. He will also help you with character development which is the main component of personal growth.

4. **Mentors offer encouragement and help keep us going**

   Your mentors are there with you no matter what. There offer moral support and motivate you to get going despite the challenges. There will be times that you will find yourself "caved-in," emotionally, or about to give up on the business. However, your mentor wouldn't let you stop and provide you with the encouragement and guidance that shall give you hope and confidence that you can do and achieve whatever is asked of you.

5. **Mentors are disciplinarians that create necessary boundaries**

    You will experience a lot of tough love from your mentor because he understands that being on the path that you are on can be challenging when it comes to self-motivation and self-discipline. He will take on this role of parent to teach you good work habits and provide the boundaries for you to work within to solidify your work ethic and sharpen your focus.

6. **Mentors are there to listen to you and your ideas without any judgements**

    While starting off you may have various ideas about what to do and what not to do. You must relay all of these to your mentor who can then help you see which ones have potential and why others would be better left alone; otherwise you might be pursuing an idea that has no legs and no destination.

7. **Mentors are advisors you can put your trust in**

    In the world of business, it can be hard to know who to trust - and that you can trust someone, especially with proprietary information or intellectual property. Since your mentor would be an objective third-party with no stake in any idea or venture, he would be happy to let you know what he thinks. You can trust that he would keep everything you tell him confidential rather than sell it to someone else or steal an idea from you.

8. **Mentors can help you make connections**

    It is a very well-known saying that connections will get you into doors that degrees won't. Playing a dual role of teacher and connector, a mentor can provide access to those within your industry that are willing to invest in your company, offer their skills and expertise, introduce you to talent that can fuel your business and help you get closer to your target audience. He can help you build opportunities that you otherwise might not have had.

9. **Mentors have the experiences and can stop you from making the mistakes that they made**

    They say that a smart person learns from the mistakes of the others. Starting a business is challenging enough, so if you can skip doing things the hard way, why wouldn't you? A mentor has been there, right where you are, and has made numerous mistakes that they can now use as a basis for helping others to skip the devastating effects of not knowing.

So, be smart. Learn from the narrative of their experience, what mistakes there are that you wouldn't want to repeat for yourselves.

10. **Mentors are priceless in more ways than one**

Typically, a mentoring relationship will grow organically through connections within your industry and network. A mentor does not do it for the money. Instead, they are driven by the satisfaction of helping another person seeking financial freedom, paying it forward from a similar experience they had when starting their own journey.

A mentor would be sharing all his experiences with you which will help you in shaping your journey as well. This is what makes your connection with the mentor a priceless one.

Having a mentor is not a sign of weakness; it shows you are smart enough and are driven enough to succeed and are ready to learn in the process by the smartest and shortest way possible which is by getting yourself a mentor.

APPOINTING EMPLOYEES

"Of the top 10 sources of innovation, employees are the only resource that you can control and access that your competitors cannot. Employees are the one asset you have that can actually be a sustainable competitive advantage."

— **Kaihan Krippendorff**

Indeed true. Employees are an asset to your business, they go in as a factor of production in the production equation in the economics.

You hire employees to get results because you cannot do it all by yourself because you do not have the time to do it all by yourself.

I know a few people get overjoyed at the mention of being the one on the hiring side. Feels like so much power, so much authority but it is a great responsibility. It is a daunting task which needs to be done with You are basically appointing someone to work in place of you to run your business. You will need them to be the best that they can be at whatever task it is that you are hiring them for.

HIRING THAT FIRST EMPLOYEE

After months of having operated your business yourself and having worn as many hats as possible at some point in your business, you will make that first hire to offer you a helping hand to keep you competitive and keep you prospering. It will be one of the biggest moments in your life and you deserve the applaud and are also allowed to celebrate but be careful to not forget that your first hire is an important hire and must be made with good amount of scrutiny.

You need to understand that hiring an extra person to work with you brings with itself a whole new rally of obligations, legal work, liabilities and expenses.

You will also need to train the hired employee to tailor their skills to the need of your company.

Hiring a mismatch can really take a toll on the well-being and reputation of your company which will still be a baby. There are certain precautions that you might want to take when making that first hire.

BE RATIONAL

You gut instinct may have never let you down but leave it outside the door when you are hiring an employee. Remember, your employee is supposed to be an asset! Don't hire a liability.

Any person who comes to you for an interview dressed in a suit is not a saint. Whether they are coming for a job where they have to maintain the finances or file reports, do the tech work or do the quantitative forecasting; know that unstable minds and criminals can hide under any uniform. I don't mean to scare you. I just mean to say that perform a rational background checks.

Most of the applications that will come to your desk will have inflated and untrue facts about the applicants.

Imagine if you hire a person to work for your company who doesn't have his ethics in place and performs and displays unethical behavior either at workplace or criminal behavior outside the workplace, who will be sued?

You might even want to conduct a social security check of the potential hire. With the applicant's consent you might want to dig up into documents which are otherwise not publicly demonstrated.

Try to obtain the original educational credentials if you can because with such great advancement in technology, forging any kind of documents have become a cake walk for everyone.

You might also want to look into their criminal past because in case they turn out to have been previously involved in some illegal activities or if they are a prison runaway (maybe that got a bit extreme). Anyway, you do not want to work with a person who has a potential of undertaking criminal and illegal activities; because guess who is going to jail with them this time? Yes, you!

Sometimes, if you are certain about who you want to hire given your requirements but still want to scrutinize into the matter; you can take the help of a third party to conduct a thorough check while also informing the person whose records you are tracking down.

SUBSTANCE ABUSE

Recreational drugs now are being used more than ever. If your potential hire is an addict, you can't expect a forever stoned or drunk person to offer you the productivity you need or be that helping hand that you're hiring them to be. Around 70% of the on-the-job accidents have been reported to be cases of drug abuse.

You need to weed out while hiring and a drug test should be somewhere near the top on the list. You can deny the offer if the potential refuses to the drug test.

Now, you have selected the person you see as most likely being hired. What next?

BE OBJECTIVE

You had asked the necessary questions and run the required background checks during the hiring process. If at all if you need to know more about the person you're hiring, remember to keep your dignity in place as well and don't ask inappropriate questions pertaining to their sexual orientations, their marital status, age, race or religion. This might come across as discriminating.

Apart from that whatever questions you are asking, keep it short and have a clear objective behind any query. You don't want to take a peek into someone's life for no reason.

COMPENSATION

Depending upon the amount of work and the status of the employee as being part time or full time, you will decide upon the remuneration that you will be dispensing unto the employee for the services he promises to render to you.

RECORDS

You might want to keep a record of the documents of your new employee. Their age, a document validating their citizenship, a contract signed with them to name a few. You need to have these in place.

The process of hiring is indeed a long process that needs to be carried out very carefully. So, now we must outline the importance of employees that validates why you should go through this cumbersome process.

EMPLOYEES MAKE OR BREAK THE BUSINESS

Motivated and empowered employees sit at the core of the success of any business. Workers are one of the most powerful assets that a company has. Business entirely depend upon their employees to achieve goals, meet deadlines, uphold quality, satisfy clients and customers.

Everyone loves a little recognition. If you give enough spotlight to a particular employee on their outstanding performance, they are bound to perform even better and also empower other employees to keep up with the tough competition. Hence, giving recognition where it is du goes a long way in empowering the employees to do better.

Also, with the right information, training and opportunities, empowered employees have the capability to complete their tasks with minimal supervision. Create the right employee culture, values-driven workplace and employee engagement, and workers will also be personally driven to take responsibility and perform well.

You are the leader and it would only pay to behave like one and as a leader you don't boss around but encourage and empower those who work with you.

EMPLOYEE INVOLVEMENT PLAYS AN IMPORTANT ROLE IN A COMPETITIVE BUSINESS ENVIRONMENT

Any business' success relies on the well-being of its employees. The employees need to be engaged with the business instead of being treated as salaried workers. As a leader, you must make them realize that they are a part of something bigger than themselves. When you ensure employee participation with the company they are bound to produce favorable results.

These are the people who actually run your business. Their active involvement is something that you cannot overlook at any cost.

With more involvement, you have more motivated employees, more motivated employees imply better results.

In an employee-centric environment, you will retain and attract talent because employees realize that they are being given the value they deserve and not being treated as a means to an end.

You started your business with a vision and goal in your mind. It can only be achieved with more efficiency if everyone is on the same page. Your business must run like a well-oiled machine which can only happen if everyone working towards the common goal is happy and in a harmonious connection with each other. When employees are well engaged they get to take a closer look at the bigger picture which makes them more motivated to work because they now know what role do they play in this bigger picture. This conviction towards a bigger goal and mission is what makes them more productive.

Any business is nothing but a piece of paper without its employees and unmotivated employees can really wreak havoc on the entire book.

Therefore, it is very crucial that you keep employee involvement an utmost priority.

INVEST IN YOUR EMPLOYEES
WHY?

Most of the employees are not happy at their workplace which makes them to work half-heartedly. When was the last time you performed an uninteresting task by tapping your potential to the fullest?

Dissatisfied employees provide inefficient results and that is something that is detrimental to the sustenance of your business.

Some companies may be micro managing their employees too much. No adult likes someone hovering over their head all the time which can make them irritated. Other companies on the opposite hand might be paying no attention to communication, guiding or training the employees assuming that they know everything about what is to be done. Companies must view communication and training as an investment rather than treating it as an expense.

A few companies go overboard with being strict; tracking the employees' every move, following a strict dress code, over hours and extra night shifts brew unhappiness in employees and they start treating work like a burden which greatly hampers their performance.

If the company in competition is winning on this part, sorry to say but it will be a winner overall. That is why happy employees are very important because happier the employees are, happier your customers will be and your business will grow exponentially. As a result of which everyone will be happy.

HOW?

Paycheck and Intangibles: It is obviously important to keep the employees' paycheck and benefits competitive in order to attract talent. But somethings extend beyond money that make you win. Employees want recognition and involvement and to know better about their leaders

Career Development: If you do not foster a learning environment in the workplace, if you do not pay enough attention to training the employees. No employee would stay to do a job they don't know how to do. By providing them the required training, you're conveying a message that you care about them in the long term and then employees are more likely to not quit.

Workplace Flexibility: Nobody ever likes a hostel like environment or a hostile environment for that matter. If you create workplace flexibility as long as your employee is delivering you results, I don't see why would your employee want to quit unless of course you are being an extremely painful "boss" in other aspects. Flexibility ensures better performance because now an employee doesn't feel like he is being treated as cattle being given fodder and asked to work according to the master.

Listen to your Employees: I can't even recall how many times through the course of this chapter have I stressed upon the importance of involvement of employees and keeping them engaged. Again, this helps them see a bigger picture and gives them an up close view of the mission ad vision that they have been working for.

Be open about the feedback from employees and always be ready to take actions upon that feedback. Remember, they are your assets and they are the ones who run your business.

Sometimes, the impeccably talented people you hire as employees can come up with ideas that can bear you and your business fruits. It wouldn't hurt to listen to them as well. There are some people who do not listen to their employees thinking that they sit on the top of the pyramid and need to listen to no one below them. Imagine what would happen if the base of that pyramid weakens?

WHAT DOES IT FEEL LIKE TO HAVE A MILLION DOLLARS!

Everyone has that million-dollar bank balance dream. If anyone ever tells you that they don't care about money, run away from them because they are lying!

It is a very well-known adage that "Money can't buy happiness but poverty can't buy anything." Isn't it true? Don't you want money? Don't you want to buy that fancy car? Don't you want to have that expensive closet? Don't you want to go on international vacations?

Can the pretense of disliking money ever get you that? Money can never be the cause of evil. Evil is the cause of evil. Those who are bad will do bad irrespective of whether money is involved or not. Who is paying a suicide bomber? But they still take a thousand innocent lives because they are evil. So, yes, I'll repeat, money is not the cause of evil. Evil is what does evil. Discussion ends here.

A million dollars is a dream that many have but only a few have the potential to turn it into reality. Actually, the truth is that everyone has the potential but a few have the courage to tap into that potential and make the most out of it.

There is no lack of motivation to become a millionaire. See any rich person around you, think of someone even richer, yes that would be a millionaire. Now, get up and get to work! You can't sit and sweat out a million dollars. Forget that you can't even sweat at all by sitting and doing nothing.

Find your passion, research, make a plan and go pursue it. This is the way to get started and once you get started the momentum to keep going generates on its own.

Make a vision board of what a million-dollar lifestyle would look like. Look at it every day until you are motivated enough to not just dream about it but to embark on the journey to becoming another success story.

Jordan Belfort in The Wolf of the Wall Street said, *"Let me tell you something. There's no nobility in poverty. I've been a poor man, and I've been a rich man. And I choose rich every f***ing time."*

And I cannot agree more! I don't even know from what place do these people who despise money come to call themselves noble from?

By now there are plenty of millionaires across the world and no one can the value of money better than these people who built it all from scratch. They respect each and every penny though they have millions to their name.

Have you ever had this experience where you liked something in a shopping mall but had to leave it because it was priced out of your affordability? Does it serve to live a full life and not work at any point to change that? Does it serve to keep walking away from everything that you like all the time just because you cannot afford it so you just accept it to be out of your league?

When was the last time you didn't turn around to praise that beautiful luxury car you saw on the road? When was the last time you didn't wish it was yours?

Imagine if you had the power to buy anything and everything you wanted? Wouldn't it all be so wonderful? No more wishing, hoping and accepting the lack? Imagine what abundance would feel like?

Money can take you places even your imagination cannot and trust me a million dollars is a lot of money and it certainly requires a lot of effort to make but is it impossible? No! People do it all the time.

There are uncountable options of becoming a millionaire and since Business Development is hue on demand it is one of the sure shot ways to become a millionaire if you are ready to put in the work. By becoming a Business Developer and being devoted to learn and to execute, even you can become a millionaire and if you put your mind to it, there is no power in the world that can stop you from getting whatever it is that you want.

Anyone can be and have what they want if they have the faith and the courage to pursue it.

Now, let's pump you up a bit more and take you through what the life of a millionaire looks like!

Having a million dollars is a very exhilarating feeling undeniably but the work never ends. There is always more to earn, more to do, more to learn. Most of the people who banked their first million may have partied for just a few hours and gotten back to work. That is how addicted must a millionaire be to his work to become and to stay a millionaire. This is because when you work your way up there, you tend to learn the value of time better.

This said, the life of a millionaire beyond work is still pretty awesome. The best part is that most millionaires are either self-employed or entrepreneurs which frees them from asking any boss for a permission to go on a vacation. Just in case work starts taking a toll on you, pack your bags and fly away. Money is anyway not a problem, right?

Once you are a millionaire, you not only improve the quality of your life but also of those who are related to you. What better a way to make your parents proud and pay them back for everything that they sacrificed for your happiness.

You can give an altogether better lifestyle to your family and again they share in your riches, now they are rich too. And who doesn't like it? No matter how flashy it might be nobody can deny the charm of having so much money in the bank that you don't even know where to spend.

Hold on! That does not mean you start spending ruthlessly. You need to keep that income coming and keep saving more than you spend, more savings again give your more money to invest hence back to more income, more money to spend, more money to save and that is how this circle in the spiral goes on. And even though you'll be saving more you will still have more than enough to spend.

A few people talk of the concept of necessity and luxury. Everyone eventually manages to acquire the basic necessities of life, after all they are necessary for survival but it doesn't harm to have the luxury of experiencing luxuries if you worked hard enough and in the right direction to earn it.

Financial stability is someone that everyone is always seeking. It can free you from the anxiety of the money problems. As a millionaire, you can go to vacations a few times a year and sometimes even travel first class. You can book whatever villa or resort or five-star that you want.

If ever you like a couture from a designer, you can afford it without giving a second thought.

Leave all that, even if there is a new car in the market, you can even buy that. Once you have more than enough money, you can even buy yourself a chopper or a private jet or a yacht too.

IS A MILLIONAIRE'S LIFE DIFFERENT?

No! Not really! They still are humans facing the same life as they did before, just improved.

A millionaire is not free from problems; his problems are just better

Instead of looking for a job you are now looking for people to whom you can offer a job. Instead of living paycheck to paycheck you now have lives that depend upon you. You are now no more worried about the increase in compensation but about the innovation and strategies that you can undertake to take your business to next level.

Money is no longer that stressful

You will always be anxious about making more money but by now you would have known the trick so it won't freak you out as much as it did earlier. You won't at least be worried about making your ends meet. You won't be worried about paying your rent or from where the money for bills will come. You will be free from trivial stresses but stress to make more will keep hovering. As a millionaire, if you learn how to manage your personal finances well, even if your business goes into a slowdown for some time, you will be able to survive without worrying about being able to meet your ends while you work on reviving your business.

Money will still be a stressor for you but the reasons will be more empowering.

Better Health

Healthcare is expensive. Most of the people who earn enough to only make their ends meet might avoid visiting a doctor even when they are slightly ill, let alone keeping a track of their health on regular basis which is actually important. A healthy mind lives in a healthy body and the healthier your mind the better you will perform at whatever work you are doing.

With more money, you can have access to better medicines, gym memberships, supplements, spa visits, scheduled check-ups.

Regular visits to dentists must always be made to keep your oral health in check. As a millionaire, you can afford those costly appointments for you as well as your family.

When you have money to invest in your health, your life changes for better.

The healthier you are, the happier you will be. You will be more energetic, more motivated and more productive; you'll work more and work better and make more money. Investment in your health is one of the best decisions you will ever make.

Even if you're broke right now, make sure you're keeping aside some money to invest in looking after your health. Once you start investing in your health, it will pay you back in ways you cannot even imagine.

You have access to better of everything when you have more money.

Better Social Groups

You are an average of the people you hang out with. As a millionaire, you have access to crowd that is more driven, and a crowd that has already achieved all that they ever wanted to.

When you are broke, you might have friends who are doing well but you will still be kind of in the same boat because birds of a feather always flock together.

When you are a millionaire, you get to attend the high class parties where you meet other millionaires, billionaires, industry experts and business moguls.

As a result of your success, you will also earn respect of your peers and have better access to influential people and high level social groups.

You could still have accessed them if you weren't a millionaire but once you have achieved success, these important people will take you far more seriously among whom you can find potential future business partners, mentors and investors.

Even though, the basic construct of your life remains the same, as a millionaire the details of the basics certainly improve.

Obviously the rich and the broke, both eat food, but getting food is the last thing that a rich person has to worry about because he has it sorted.

Similarly, on the whole the rich and the broke might be doing the same thing to survive but, once you dig deeper, being rich is better than being broke any day and the hard work you have to put in to make that cash, will be worth it all.

HOW GOOGLE ADWORDS WORK

Anyone who has a little knowledge of how the marketing of business works, must have surely heard of Google AdWords, popularly known as Google Ads. Google ads evolved as Google's major source of revenue.

Directly from the dictionary, Google AdWords is an advertising service developed by Google to help the marketers reach their customers instantly. The advertisers pay to display the brief advertisements, product listings and service offerings. The adverts appear on the Google **Search Engine Results Page.**

When someone searches for a term on Google, google throws in a list of results and if you would notice that the topmost and the bottom most results are ads. These are the Google Ads.

TYPES OF GOOGLE ADWORDS

Search Ads

If a searcher searches for something on Google, a listing of ads will appear just above the list of organic results that show up. For Example: If you search for "violin teachers", the first few results will be from a few maestros who will be found promoting themselves via Google ads in search for some students.

However, there are a few factors as those listed below that influence which results will be displayed first.

Targeting: This includes specifying the geographic location where you want to promote your ad. This is usually done by specifying a zip code.

Search term and keyword: In this case the marketer analyzes the keyword that a potential customer is most likely to make a search with. The marketer can optimize this keyword for the ad.

Ad Relevance: The ads that are being displayed on the search engine results page must be relevant to what the person was looking for. An attempt to search for violin teachers must not yield results for math teachers. It would make no sense.

Landing Page Experience: How relevant is the landing page to what the searcher wanted? Did he get what he was looking for?

Conversion Rate: This is again dependent upon relevance, landing page experience and experience that the user has after clicking on that ad.

Bid: If two advertisers are at par with regards to the above factors then the advertiser that offers the higher bid is the one that gets the preference.

Quality Score: The quality score really depends upon the above factors combined. It is all interrelated.

Another kind of ads that can be run in search network are

1. **Call-only ads** – This ad is available only on call enabled mobile devices. After clicking the ad, instead of taking you to a landing page, you make a call directly.

2. **Dynamic ads** – This ad type is more suitable for businesses who have a well-managed website. This is because the content of the ad as well as the landing pages is taken from the website. They are very similar to text ads, except that no keywords are involved here. A user searches for "violin courses". Google displays a list of ads. But dynamic ads would automatically replace the ad headline with "violin course" and the ad text with the relevant website content and landing page".

3. **Mobile app promotion** – These ads are suitable for businesses with mobile applications that are installed and run. The goal of this ad is to encourage users to download your app or take a desired action within the app. For Example: Amazon.

Display Ads

You must have noticed them while you are reading a post or viewing a video on some random website, you must have seen ads in a lot of different places on the page, and in different dimensions. These are display ads. There are images of the product or services the marketer is promoting.

Here the searcher is not explicitly looking for what the ad offers. But, these ads are displayed based on a number of factors like keywords, audience interest, managed placements to name a few. These display ads only appear on advertising-supported websites.

Below are the targeting criteria, based on which Google selects the websites to place and prioritize the banner ads.

Keywords – The ads are displayed based on the keywords that they are optimized for. Let's say the keyword for the ad is "Business Development", then Google would choose websites that have content on the topic.

Placements – Placements are nothing but the websites on which you want your ad to appear. You will just need to add the websites where you want to show the ads, instead of keywords. For example, if you want to show your ads only on automobile related websites, then look for advertising supported automobile sites and add them to your targeting.

Remarketing – This helps you reconnect with your existing website visitors. Using this, you can target visitors who have come to your website but have not taken any action.

You basically got an audience when they first visited the website and now are just putting up the show for them again and again to convince them better.

Topic – There are specific topics in AdWords, under which all websites are grouped. It will be easier for the advertisers to choose topics related to the businesses. For example, websites related to automobiles will be listed under the topic 'automobiles.'

Shopping Ads

Have you ever been in need of shoes and just went to Google and searched for "blue shoes"? Have you seen how on the top of the page there are images for blue shoes from various retailers and if you click on those you are directed directly to the shopping website. These are called shopping ads.

This campaign type would make more sense for a retailer like Amazon or Asos or any other app. This ad type boosts traffic to the website and helps in generating quality leads as well as increasing the conversions.

Video Ads

This ad type lets the advertisers run their ads either on YouTube or other Google display networks. You must have noticed ads in the middle of your favorite YouTuber's videos. These are the video ads we are talking about.

Benefits of running video ads

Better targeting – This ad type has demographic, location, interest, keyword and device targeting which helps you reach the right audience on YouTube and Google Display Network. You certainly want to put your resources to the best use so you must focus on targeting and Google AdWords do that for you.

Better reach – YouTube is one of the most visited websites and has around 30 million visitors every day. You can now gauge for yourself you diverse and huge in number your reach can be.

Video ads are also available on Google Display Network. This means that you are more likely to have an access to a wider and more diverse audience.

Measurable – Unlike advertising on TV, YouTube ads let you know all the necessary metrics like views, view rate, clicks, reach and frequency, engagement, performance etc. This helps you measure the success of video ads which can further help you in creating ads in future analyzing these statistics.

Universal App Ads

This campaign is helpful for businesses with a mobile app. Here, the advertiser can promote the mobile app across search, Play Store, Display & YouTube. AdWords uses ad text ideas and other assets right from the app store listings. All you need to do is provide some text, a budget, and a starting bid. Also, it is important to set languages and locations for the ad. By utilizing all this information, AdWords itself designs a variety of ads in different formats. Google will itself test different ad combinations and display the one that performs the best.

BENEFITS OF USING GOOGLE ADWORDS

Now that we have learnt all about what Google ads are, there should also be a reason why you would want to use this tool to boost your business. So, now we will discuss all the benefits that are of using Google Ads.

1. **AdWords work faster than SEO**

    The topmost benefit of Google AdWords is that it works faster than SEO. Both SEO and Google AdWords are search engine marketing strategies to generate more traffic and leads. But, a well optimized AdWords campaign can work much more efficiently for a business to get the much coveted higher spot on the SERP. AdWords are faster and more effective because

- You can work with **multiple keywords** at a time.
- You can **turn the campaign on or off** whenever you wish to.
- Ads which appears on the top of the page get immediate **visibility**.

Of course, this does not mean that you should overlook organic sources, as they have more long-term benefits. But with AdWords, there is a definite better chance of driving more traffic and leads instantly. Additionally, the platform is more transparent, and you know exactly what is happening with the ads.

On the other hand, search engine optimization, though effective, is a long-term process. To rank for any keyword, it requires a lot of perseverance and a lot of well-written articles, and backlinks. And even after all that, it will take a while for them to gain the necessary authority.

Simply put, ads give you instant visibility at an instant cost, whereas SEO would give you long term success, depending on the effort you put on the quality of your content.

You might need to use both simultaneously, but be aware about the success time frame, and the effort and money that would be needed for both.

2. **Increase brand awareness**

    Google AdWords, aside of boosting traffic, clicks, and conversions; is also an efficient way to educate people about your brand. To verify this theory, Google partnered with Ipsos to run a study across 12 verticals, from automobiles to retail. It was discovered that search ads increase awareness by an average of 6.6%.

    When it comes to SEO, your rank also depends on the number of your brand name searches. That's an important reason as to why you should aim to increase brand awareness through search, as well as display ads.

3. **Reach more customers through their Gmail Inbox**

    One of the most used marketing strategies is email marketing, which is why Gmail ads can be extremely helpful. In 2015, Google integrated native Gmail ads with Google AdWords and made it available to all advertisers, which means you can reach out to more prospects through their Gmail inbox.

Usually, Gmail ads appear on the promotion tab, and sometimes you can see it on the social tab too. These ads run both on desktops and mobiles. Gmail ads generally cost much less than search ads and so if you have a smaller budget, then you must try Gmail ads as well.

4. **Track the performance**

It is very difficult to measure the outcome and reach of traditional advertisements like newspapers, radio, broadcast television, cable television, outdoor billboards, brochures etc.

You wouldn't know the source of the leads coming from these media, unless your customer chooses to share it. As a result, it would be very difficult to calculate the ROI you got from traditional media.

AdWords, on the other hand, would tell you exactly what happened with the campaign. You would know who clicked on your ad, how many leads have been generated, how much traffic you attracted was from AdWords to your website, which keyword was most efficient in generating the most traffic and leads and how much does it cost you per lead.

This would help marketers understand what works and what doesn't. Using this information, you can then re-design your campaigns so as to achieve optimal results.

5. **Tackle your competition better**

When someone searches for something related to your product or services online, and you aren't running ads, but your competitors are, then they sure have an upper hand and you'll lose business to them almost instantly.

You need to keep an eye on them to see how they are promoting their business like they tell you to keep your friends close and enemies closer. The transparent system of Google AdWords helps you keep a track on the kind of and amount of ads that they are running. Make the best of this opportunity and make yourself stand out against your competition.

To sum up everything we discussed in this chapter, I don't see a reason why an efficient and a goal oriented marketer wouldn't run Google Ads.

USE FACEBOOK TO YOUR ADVANTAGE

Can one miss the ever so popular social media website like Facebook? We all had had so much fun during our teens with Facebook.

Would you ever wonder Facebook is one of the best places to promote your business? You are bound to be losing out on the lot of potential that Facebook has to offer in boosting your sales of whatever product or service it is that you are looking to sell?

Every business, small or big, should be on Facebook. It boasts of approximately 1.71 billion monthly users; businesses can use Facebook in quite a few ways to promote their business and earn their business some recognition.

Facebook knows a lot about its users and is therefore one of the best tools to target a specific audience through paid campaigns.

For the past years, as discussed through earlier chapters, Google and Social Media sites have become an important tool for business owners to market and advertise their products and services. When it comes to social media, Facebook is one of the most used websites in the world and Social Media Marketing occupies a significantly important space in the Business Development.

Using Facebook is a part of people's daily routine; they post, like, and share the things they want to see and what others connected with their accounts would want to see.

As Facebook continues to grow by the day, they expanded their reach by launching 'Facebook Marketplace' in 2016. This feature was basically for entrepreneurs and business owners to get the chance to sell their products online, and for business owners who have their own page, Facebook also added a feature for e-commerce. With a focused and strategic approach, advertising on Facebook has an enormous marketing potential for any business; big or small.

However, marketing on Facebook benefits small business owners and retailers the most.

Small businesses offer more unique products and services to a smaller range of customers and Facebook provides an excellent opportunity to reach the exact specific target audience with a personal approach because Facebook knows about the behavior of its users. Facebook allows you to find, define and understand the demographics for your product. When you know who your customers are, you're able to provide the right audience with the right product or services best suited to their needs which will obviously improve your conversion rate.

Moreover, to be perfect at small-business marketing on Facebook, you don't need to run an IT company. Internet marketing for small business is that it allows you to compete with larger businesses.

If you offer a niche product or service, you might even have some competitive and comparative advantage. A large business does not really have the time to focus in depth on a single niche.

FACEBOOK MARKETING

Facebook marketing is done by creating—and actively using a Facebook page as a communications channel to maintain contact with and attract customers. Facebook provides for this by allowing users to create individual profiles or business pages for companies, organizations, or any group looking to create and grow a fan base for a product, service, or a brand.

Having aboard nearly a billion potential customers, every business should be using Facebook. It is at least as important as having a business web page. The best part is that Facebook pages are easier to create. Whether you represent a big brand or a small business, there's a guarantee that some portion of your customers are already on Facebook.

HOW DOES FACEBOOK MARKETING WORK?

A business page can be searched for as soon as it is up, but unlike a personal profile, you cannot invite friends through it. Business pages do not get "friends," they get "followers".

To create an initial seed for the fan base, marketing team begins by liking the business page on their own personal profiles. When an individual likes a page, Facebook immediately advertises this event to their profile and this activity can be seen by every one of their friends which can make them click on your page and browse through your services.

Every Facebook user who likes a page will get to see any content that that business page posts, and will be notified of posts on their news feed. If they are engaged by that content, the activity appears on all of *their* friends' news feeds. The company›s task, is to encourage this process as much as possible.

The most important aspect of Facebook marketing is consistency of communication. Creating a Facebook page and then leaving it alone will bring a business nothing. To attract followers, a business should regularly post new content in a variety of different formats, so that more people will see, engage with and share the content which will make it to reach more people.

Content can be to announce upcoming promotions, specific products, share fun facts, provide incentive codes for discounts on products and services, and anything else that catches the attention of the followers.

Given the way Facebook's news feed works, how recent the post is, is a major factor in deciding what a user sees. An average user has more than 100 friends, and may be following several other brands and pages as well. There is no way to instantly see all the activity from every one of those sources.

The news feed shows them posts which are more recent. Therefore, a company's post is only likely to be visible on their followers' news feeds for about three hours after they post it. Therefore, you must analyze the time of the day and the day of the week when most of your followers are active on their feeds and post your content accordingly to have it reach maximum people and to reap maximum benefits from the content you worked so hard on.

Invite your followers to engage with your content because the more the engagement with the content, the more the visibility and hence, more is the reach. Since the content that you share on Facebook can be in the form of texts or images or videos, you can have really good interaction with your followers.

Such low-commitment investments encourage familiarity and affinity in their customer base.

This positive relationship can be made advantageous through maintaining a two-way communication. When fans post a comment on content, businesses should respond because the more any particular fan interacts with a page, the more likely he or she is to buy.

HOW TO MAKE THE MOST OF FACEBOOK?

We know that Facebook is a really powerful tool to use for promoting your business but there should be a lot of people using it for marketing then, including your competitors. To have a proper strategy in place will always give you an upper hand over your competition.

POST WITH INTENT: You can't just throw irrelevant and random stuff on your business page in the name of content and expect to attract customers. There should be an intention behind every post that you make which aligns with the goals that you had in mind when you created the page.

ENGAGE: It is utterly important for you to engage with the people you are involved with, be it customers, clients or employees. Here, make sure that the content you are posting is not to monotonous and an in-your-face promotion of the product. Post contests and quizzes to increase interaction with your followers to attract their attention in your page by keeping them entertained.

PLAN: Have a content calendar that will help you plan better upon the content you are going to post. A content calendar is the best way to maximize your output with the posts because once you have the calendar in place you can focus better on the quality of the content you will now be sharing. Furthermore, you can use applications like Sprout Social to schedule your posts.

BE CONSISTENT WITH YOUR FACEBOOK STORIES: Stories are a good way to constantly show up on your followers feed. You can even afford to be little casual with the content you post on the stories, by which I mean to say that you do not necessarily have to post content that resonates with your service. You can post anything fun and interesting. The goal is to keep constantly showing up on your followers' feed which will increase the visits to your actual page.

QUALITY OVER QUANTITY: Though you want to be consistent with your page and not just disappear in thin air but do not obsess over the frequency of posts so much that you have to compromise with the quality of the content that you are posting and end up sharing just anything. That being said, with lesser number of posts you can work with smaller budget when using paid promotions.

BOOST YOUR POSTS: Facebook allows you to pay for the promotion of your post. You can boost your post and that will widen the reach of your post and make it visible to a larger audience some of which can convert into your new followers.

POWER EDITOR TOOL: It is a bulk ads creation tool used by advertisers. It has some really cool tools that can help you promote posts and generate ads.

STRUCTURE THE PIXEL: Pixel collects data about who is visiting your website and helps you target those consumers later. Smart brands do whatever it takes to make conversion tracking, optimization and remarketing easier. Pixel is the perfect tool for doing so. It helps you find new customers who are similar to your website visitors.

TEST AD PLACEMENTS: There are different placements for ads available with Facebook. Try both the Newsfeed and right-hand-side ads to see what performs best. Results however prove that though the right-hand side ads might be cheaper than newsfeed ads, they may not get you the desired amount of clicks or conversions.

LINK RETARGETING: If you're using Facebook retargeting ads to attract visitors to your website, you should use link retargeting, too. This facilitates you to build out your retargeting lists and reach audiences that haven't visited your website before but have been influenced by your brand on social media.

Basically, link retargeting allows you to add Facebook retargeting pixels to your short link when sharing curated content. Anyone who clicks on this content can be retargeted with relevant ads even if the link led them to a third-party website.

POWER OF ECONOMICS

Business and Economics are inseparables. One really makes no sense without another. The performance of the business is closely related to the Economic cycle and the performance of the businesses is also the factor that in some way gives rise to the Economic cycle.

A smart businessman knows the market and for that he must understand the economics of the market.

One thing that micro economics teaches you very well is the Consumer Behavior. A smart businessman also knows the behavior of his customers and manipulates his services accordingly to the benefit of one and all. Therefore, since Economics boils down to the study of human behavior, knowing the principles of economics can come in really handy for a Business Developer.

Economics generates relationships between the government, the society, the private and the public organizations. All of these need to co-exist in harmony for the economy as well as for businesses to thrive.

BUSINESS ECONOMICS

Business economics is generally applied microeconomics. It bridges the business gap that exists between business practices and economic theories. It uses tools of logical science, mathematics, decision science, and economics. These concepts are deployed in taking rational and optimal business decisions which is why the name, "business economics."

Business economics integrates theories of economics with business practice. In short, business economics is a decision making science with some mathematics involved.

Though your business might really be affected by the macro economic situation of the country, scope of business economics is narrower than the entire curriculum of pure economics, it mostly encompasses the tools of microeconomics.

Theories of Business Economics are related to the study of economic activities of a firm. It provides knowledge of how a firm uses traditional economic theories into practice. Business economics reduces the gap between abstract economic theory and business practice. Business

Economics provides a link between economic theory and decision science in the analysis and decision making process of the business.

Considering the economic state of the country or even the world for that matter might make sense to a lot of people because if the economy is in a slowdown, businesses will stop making profits and might even need to be shut down. However, when it comes to decision making, a lot of people go by their gut instinct instead of taking calculated decisions. These people do not realize the power and importance of Business Economics. Believe it or not, tools of Business Economics go into the working of your business long before you commence your business in full swing and you will need to deploy it throughout the journey of your business should you be intending to see your business thrive to its complete potential.

Let's see in detail why inclusion of Business Economics in Decision Making is unavoidable

1. **It covers demand analysis and forecasting**

    Demand analysis is always crucial in identifying the different factors that often influence the demand for the product of the firm because that is how you are going to determine the supply you are going to come out with. It also offers guidelines on how to manipulate demand. Normally, the core area of business decision making relies on an accurate estimate of what the demand in the market would be.

    Forecasting is a critical topic that is studied in business economics. It is usually done with econometric tools or regression analysis. Each business enterprise progresses in its process of production based on the demand anticipation for its products in the future so that it does not create excess supply which might force the business owner to reduce the prices. A market survey is conducted and research is done with a view to understanding the fashions, tastes, and preferences of consumers. Business economics usually analyzes the behavior of the demand and predicts the quantity that would be demanded by the consumers.

2. **Helps in cost analysis**

    Business economics often handles the analysis of various costs that business firms incur. Every business always desires to minimize their costs in order to maximize its profits by utilizing different economies of scale. Nonetheless, the firms fail to determine exact costs that are involved in the production process and therefore are unable to make a decision about capital budgeting and capital rationing. Therefore, it is very important for business owner to have a clear idea of the costs that will be involved because no one has infinite amounts of investment to pour into their business. Business economics often deals with the cost estimates and offers knowledge to the business people concerning cost analysis of their enterprise.

3. **Profit analysis**

   Most firms desire to gain maximum profits, however, they often experience risk and uncertainty in getting the maximum profits. There could also be an uncertainty of whether the business will make any profits at all or at what stage will it start making profits. Knowing beforehand through tools of business economics can prepare the business owner to deal with the outcome that might be. The business has to come up with new innovations in marketing and production of its products. Business economics handles issues regarding profit analysis such as profit policies, techniques and even the break down the analysis.

4. **Capital management, budgeting and rationing**

   Business economics covers capital management where it further denotes control and planning of expenditure of capital in a business firm. If the firm is undertaking more than one business operations, it might need to ration the available capital among the prospective ventures. It normally covers areas such as rate of return, selection of best project, cost of capital, net present value, profitability index and evaluation among other topics.

5. **It covers and determines production analysis**

   One feature of factors of production is that they are normally scarce and usually have alternative uses. Products based businesses might need to use these metrics in their production process. In most cases, producers combine these factors of production in a certain way in the production process to accomplish maximum output with minimum cost. Sometimes these companies might also be looking for vertical acquisition of another company that usually deals with the raw materials. Even in this case an analysis would be required and Business Economics would do the job well enough. Business economics sheds more light concerning factor productivity, production function, least cost inputs combination among others.

6. **Price determination and its techniques**

    Appropriate pricing decisions normally influence on how a firm can maximize its profits. Overprice the product and you may lose business, Underprice the product and you may fail at covering your costs. Business economics deals with techniques of price determination under various categories of market structures. Other topics related to price determination and their methods that are covered by business economics are not limited to pricing objectives, price discrimination or pricing methods.

7. **Influences the objectives of a business firm**

    It is a fact that each and every business enterprise has an objective to achieve. A firm should ensure that its objectives and methodologies should align with the way business wants to accomplish its goals. The objectives of a business often offer a precise guideline to the owner of the business while he focuses on making informed decisions about its output and price.

    The objectives of the firm mostly are that of sales maximization, profit maximization, consumer satisfaction maximization, utility maximization among other objectives. Business economics normally covers theories concerning the objectives of a business organization and to help the business owner keep up with those objectives.

8. **Business environment**

    It goes without saying that the business environment always has a significant effect on the activities and performance of business organizations. Business economics usually studies about several categories of business environment inclusive of business phase cycle, capital market and situation of money, market structure among critical topics. Business environment and business economics are complementary to each other.

There has now been a new trend about the integration of operation research and business economics, where methods like inventory models, linear programming, the game theory are regarded as part of important areas to study in business economics. Therefore, business economics is a very important element that allows most organizations and individuals to accomplish their goals in a very calculated manner and make analytical decisions.

GAIN EXPOSURE OF DIFFERENT MARKETS

As a Business Developer, though you perform diverse tasks within the same firm, you might want to spread your wings to a variety of industries as well. To gain exposure of different markets is one of the best ways to popularize your business and take it to next level and get more number of clients because now you are not limited to a specific sector or nationality. You are now ready to serve clients from various walks, races and interests.

Making a decision to expand your reach to varied industries whether domestically or internationally can be a tough one but it reaps enormous benefits nonetheless. It will require for you to learn about the different industries. Also, if you plan to glow global, you might want to be familiar with the legal and financial implications in the country you plan to expand your business to.

BENEFITS OF GAINING EXPOSURE

International Exposure

If you are planning to go global, this tough decision is going to be a blessing in disguise. Keeping your business local or even national can limit your potential for profit. Typical downsides companies face when they operate in only one country include various types of exposure to risk that increase a company's vulnerability to the market. There are different types of exposure that can limit a company's bottom line:

Transaction exposure deals with the converting of foreign money. This can be beneficial to the company if is located somewhere where the foreign currency is valued more than the domestic currency or vice versa.

Economic exposure involves exchange rate changes that can affect the company both positively and negatively. If the domestic currency depreciates, an inflow of income can be advantageous to you.

Translation exposure also involves exchange rates, but specifically, the impact of translating foreign currency to the domestic currency. Through careful timing, this can lead to a boost in reported profits or increased tax liability.

Tax exposure is the income tax obligation incurred due to collecting revenue in a foreign currency.

Risks are involved in every step that you will take throughout the journey of your business but you can always tackle through them and emerge successful. All four of these exposures coincide with one another and can greatly benefit companies if managed effectively.

New Markets

If you are planning to expand your services to different industries, you might want to educate yourself about the requirements and regulations of those industries. Before taking your business to varied markets, it is important that you research the market you are entering. Naturally, new markets can boost revenues, but they can also be detrimental to your already established business if not properly understood. You'll want to make sure what you're offering meets a need in that industry. In addition, you will need to research your new competitors and understand their strategies well too. If both the market and competitive environment seem like a good fit for your company and if you are ready to take on the challenge, then expansion can be an absolute win for you. Even with new and different competition, it can still be worth the risk for many businesses because in businesses risk and return are complementary to one another. And if competition is limited, your company may have even better opportunities than at your home industry because the barriers to entry are minimized by the absence of risk in absence of competition.

Relationships with Additional Companies

When you're conducting business, networking is key. In a diversified market, even more value should be placed on building positive relationships with other companies and industry experts. Another benefit of this diversification can be that now all of your eggs are not in one basket, therefore if sometime one industry is going in slump, you can still manage to attract clients from others. One minute you might be entering into a lucrative contract with a great new customer; the next, that customer could be going out of business putting your own company at risk in the process.

The best way to guard against this risk is to diversify your business and expand into new markets. Relationships with international suppliers and distributors, or with other companies from your country, can be an incredible resource for your company. Moreover, companies often find that competing with companies from different industries can help them be more successful in their own original industry by gaining new business ideas.

Faster Growth

Expanding your company domestically or internationally naturally provides opportunities for faster growth. Researching a market properly is a critical first step. Product demand fluctuates over time. This can be beneficial for a company setting their sights on spreading their services. Sometimes, expanding to a new market helps address that fluctuation. Even at the earlier stage of their businesses, one should consider whether the need they are serving in their home market might be a need to new buyers as well. If so, expansion can directly translate to higher profit and revenue.

Business Rejuvenation

In addition to expanding a thriving business, entering new markets can help revive a struggling enterprise or an enterprise looking to increase its revenues. Businesses operating in a saturated market or experiencing a shrinking market share can find new favorable opportunities for their products and services in another market or another country. If the recognition in the original market is less, the business owner might want to expand to the new market to get their well-deserved success.

New Revenue Potential

By diversifying your business, you get access to a much larger base of customers. If your product or service is a success, you can enjoy increased revenues from these new customers even if you have saturated your markets. Diversification and Globalization could be exactly the shot of life your company needs to take its revenues to new heights.

Reach More People

The solutions your business offers undoubtedly have the potential to help your customers improve their own businesses or lives in some way. When you take your business to different markets, you can help an exponentially greater number of people find the answers to the questions or challenges your company helps with.

Greater Access to Talent

Another excellent benefit of diversification is that you get access to a new pool of potential employees with unique skills and mindsets, which gives you an edge on other organizations in your field.

Learning a New Industry

Getting information about a new industry or a new country can help make your organization more well-rounded. It will give you a new perspective on relations with customers, and may even help you work better with your previous customers and business partners.

Exposure to Foreign Investment Opportunities

Foreign investment can be extremely valuable for your business as many companies already know. If you plan to take your company global you gain an access to foreign investment opportunities which have in them the potential to give you insane returns.

When you go global, you can more easily learn about these investment opportunities and how beneficial they can be for your company and your net worth as well.

Company's Reputation

Businesses that can successfully diversify and market their services to a totally different clientele and serve them well will enjoy the prestige that they will earn from having achieved this. It is not an easy feat to accomplish, meaning prospects and potential business partners will instantly think more highly of your company when they know you have both diverse and international presence.

After all, we are here to make an impression too along with making money!

WHAT MAKES OR BREAKS A COMPANY

Everyone dreams of being their own boss someday, of working on their own schedule and of not having to work under someone else or take orders from someone else. Owning a business is very appealing to people for various and obvious reasons. But all good things do not come easy and there is nothing easy about being an entrepreneur either. Not everyone is cut to be an entrepreneur; not because they lack skills but because they lack conviction.

Being an entrepreneur is a lot of freedom from the regular 9-5 but takes insane amounts of work more than the 9-5 too. You have to wear a lot of hats to be a successful entrepreneur, you need to be a good leader, a good manager and a great decision maker. It takes more than just guts to start your own business, get it going and being your own boss.

Apart from the seed capital, a lot of emotional and physical investment needs to be made into starting and creating a successful business. The journey can sometimes get lonely too. So, an entrepreneur needs to be rational and headstrong too.

Often, first time entrepreneurs jump right into starting their own business without acknowledging the factors that shall go into making it actually run. It takes a lot more than putting in money and working meager or even working hard but with no direction.

It certainly is the flashy life that you see on TV, but what they don't show you is the intense grind that happens behind the scenes. You will have to work more than 100 hours in a week and be self-motivated enough to do that because now there is no boss to whom you have to answer and not everyone is so driven to work for themselves by themselves without having someone constantly remind them that they need to do the work.

Even after you have started your own company and you have got it running smooth on its wheels, you have to take care of it for the lifetime because no matter how successful, one wrong decision can lead to the doom of your company and make all that hard work go to waste and once you go from being one to being zero, building it all again can be a very tough and a very depressing journey.

So, what does it take to start a successful business and to keep it running successfully

1. **Be Innovative**

   If you want to survive and thrive, especially in a competitive industry, you need to determine what makes you stand out from the competitors. Clever marketing alone won›t guarantee that your target customers will be wowed by what you're offering and will buy into it, you have to offer something different from what your competitors already are.

   The market will dictate whether your business will succeed and one way to have the odds in your favor is to have an innovative product or service that will be well-received by the people in the market. You don't have to completely reinvent something you just have to make it better and different.

2. **The right team**

   The long-term success of your business requires that you have the right kind of talent working as a team in the process of building your brand. Your team is the company's backbone, and one toxic person can completely take your progress off the rails. Whatever the task you are building the workforce for, the pre requisite is that the right talent with the same vision and objectives will amplify the chances of success.

   Building a business requires a tremendous amount of work, especially during the startup phase. Long hours and the up-and-down roller coaster ride is much more stress-free when the entire team is willing to push hard to accomplish goals and hit milestones together.

3. **Connections and Network**

   Building a personal network of like-minded entrepreneurs has uncountable benefits. It gives you an opportunity for when you have questions or want advice to find sound help, especially in the early stages of a business. As your network grows, so do your resources and so does your business. Your network contributes to your success more than you think it does. Every business, big or small should make time to build strong, loyal and long-lasting networks.

4. **Put in the work, Hard and Smart**

   If you're not willing to get your hands dirty you might as well not even start. A lot of potential entrepreneurs have a false idea of what it's really like to own a business. They think it is just cold hard cash, flashy cars and huge mansions. Like I said before, sure it is fancy as shown in the TV but the behind the scenes is the real deal, it can be grueling and most people are not ready to do that. You have to be willing to put the work in if you want to be successful.

   Then some people work too hard and in all the wrong directions or they like to take what is called the "long route" to success. There is no short cut to success, but with your smart work combined with hard work you can smoothen out the long road and the journey won't be as rocky.

5. **Make Sales**

   Coming out with an innovative and unique product or service and making no sales doesn't equal to not having any product at all. It is worse, because you have put your resources into it and gotten nothing out of it. You might as well not have started at all in the first place. There is one thing that will quickly prove the viability of your product or service and that is the sales that you are making. Not only do sales prove you have something that provides value, but it also brings revenue into your business which is the sole reason why anybody starts a business.

   You're constantly selling your vision to current and prospective employees, partners, investors and advisors, you're constantly selling your product to the customers and the clients. The success of your business depends upon the sales that you are making, because if you are not making sales, you are being sold. Ideas can be great, but without sales to accompany them they are as good as nothing. Entrepreneurs who are great at sales give their business an edge a competitive advantage and are more likely to succeed.

WHAT TO AVOID?

It is important to know what is to be done but it is also important to know what is not to be done. If you are not focused on avoiding the mistakes, no matter how hard you work towards success, you are likely to fail. The following are what you need to take care of when running a business to prevent your hard established business from falling apart.

1. **Not having a thorough research**

    Before you launch a business, you need to do research first and after your business has taken flight, you need to keep researching on how to keep it running. Not taking time to research is one of the worst business mistakes you can make. Find out the scope of market for your product and find out how you need to make alterations to get going.

    After you have conducted enough research, design and modify your model accordingly

2. **Being unrealistic**

    After you research your market, you need to come up with a realistic plan and realistic expectations for your business. You cannot set unrealistic goals that cannot be achieved because it is going to tamper your self-confidence and that is something you cannot afford to do. Nothing can be better than being ambitious but we all know that there is no way an irrational but ambitious man can survive to the top. Unreal expectations will cause you to make bad choices and result in inflated projections and disappointment.

    When you set goals and make sales projections, think about what is reasonably possible for your business to do in the given time frame.

3. **Underestimating expenses**

    Starting a business requires a lot of capital input. Many business owners spend more money than the business brings in which results in straight losses. Running out of money could force you to close your business. Not estimating cost ahead of time is a common mistake that business owners tend to make. As a business owner you also need to be intelligent enough to weigh the opportunity cost of a decision before you decide to go all in with a certain proposition.

    Some business owners make over estimates of sales projections and spend money according to those projections. Because the projections are too generous, the business spends more than it actually brings in, causing a negative cash flow which equates to losses, and if your company is unable to cover the fixed costs, you might need to close down.

4. **Being a know it all**

   Let's be real, no one in the world can do everything on their own without taking help. Some people however feel embarrassed asking for help which is a very silly thing to do. Just accept it!

   You do not know everything that you need to know to start and run a business. No one does! Sure, you can learn things, but that takes time and time is money, you don't want to lose it. Acknowledge and accept when you don't know how to do something, and then find someone who can do it. Not asking people for help and letting your ego stand in the way is a huge business mistake. Decide for yourself, which is a bigger embarrassment? Asking for help or shutting down the business?

   If you try to learn everything yourself, you will lose a lot of valuable time and as a result, you'll be slow starting out and make mistakes along the way. When you ask for assistance from someone who knows better, you can avoid mistakes and save time and money.

5. **Ignoring marketing**

   You're proud of your business idea, but never let yourself think your idea is so good that people will themselves come to you. You have to market correctly to get your customers. Every business needs marketing because without marketing no one will know you exist.

   Try different types of marketing tools to find out what works best for your business. Use flyers, mail, and billboards, social media marketing with one or multiple accounts. Create a website and have an email signup so you can do email marketing. A business without marketing is going to go nowhere.

6. **Your market disappeared**

   With the changes in the economic cycle, the markets face fluctuations and so does your business. If management didn't take precautions to prepare for the upcoming shift; the business will suffer greatly at the hands of an uncertainty you knew was coming but were not prepared for.

7. **You and your team are not driven**

   Many entrepreneurs thrive on the challenging risk of starting something new. After the fast-paced growth period is over and the business model begins to work, entrepreneurs get overconfident and lose the excitement to work harder. Some even let monotony take over the need of putting more work in your business. Your passion needs to stay constant to persevere even after you have started seeing success. Constantly find new things about your business to keep your team and yourself interested to keep the spark alive.

8. **Toxic people around**

   One dirty fish makes the whole ocean stale. Business is team work and you must make sure that the team is free from any toxic elements hampering the peace and hence the productivity. You need to be surrounded with positive people that keep the morale high and are not demotivating, inexperienced and simply difficult to bear with.

9. **You're not making money**

   While it may seem unimaginable to give up on the business you've invested so much time and capital in, you have to know when to cut your losses. If your business is not making money, there is no point in carrying on with the same strategies. Did you start your business to not make money?

   All in all, whatever the problem might be, before shutting down, identify the problem and determine whether it's controllable. If it isn't controllable, do a thorough review of why the business failed but if there still is scope to save your business from falling flat, develop a plan of action and stick to it. If after trying everything, your business still can't be saved, determine exactly where you went wrong. Remember that lesson the next time you decide to start the business.

ARTIFICAL INTELLIGENCE

Hey Alexa! Artificial Intelligence is more common as a part of our daily lives than what people assume it to be. While artificial intelligence's acceptance in mainstream society is a new phenomenon, it is not a new concept.

"Artificial intelligence" is a broad and general term that refers to any type of computer software that engages in humanlike activities, including learning, planning and problem-solving.

MACHINE LEARNING: Machine learning is one of the most common types of artificial intelligence in development for business purposes today. Machine learning is primarily used to process large amounts of data quickly. Deep learning is an even more specific version of machine learning that relies on neural networks to engage in nonlinear reasoning. Deep learning is used to perform more advanced functions, such as fraud detection. It can do this by analyzing a wide range of factors at once.

Deep learning has a great deal of promise in business. Older machine learning algorithms tend to plateau in their capability once a certain amount of data has been captured, but deep learning models continue to improve their performance as more data is received. This makes deep learning models far more scalable and detailed and efficient to use.

ARTIFICIAL INTELLIGENCE AND BUSINESSES

Rather than serving as a replacement for human intelligence and ingenuity, artificial intelligence is generally seen as a supporting tool to enhance the efficiency of human workforce. Although artificial intelligence currently has a difficult time completing commonsense tasks in the real world, it is adept at processing and analyzing huge amounts of data far more quickly than a human brain could. Humans can then use this analysis in making their business decisions.

Artificial intelligence is also changing customer relationship management (CRM) systems. Software like Salesforce or Zoho requires heavy human intervention to remain up to date and accurate but with the help of artificial intelligence to these platforms, a normal CRM system transforms into a self-updating, auto-correcting system that stays on top of your relationship management for you. Therefore, AI can be beneficial to you and your business in more ways than one.

HOW ARTIFICAL INTELLIGENCE WILL INFLUENCE BUSINESSES FOR GOOD

Let's see how artificial intelligence can help you achieve your business goals.

Machine Learning

Machine learning is the science of designing and applying various algorithms that can learn things from past cases. For example, complex algorithms can analyze a past case and can even manage such situations beforehand. But if there are no previous cases, these algorithms won't work. By pairing artificial intelligence in business, the program won't be limited to the computer instruction that the programmer wrote. It will be more flexible and will require less regulation than traditional programs. Artificial intelligence will change the way the software behaves and adapt it to the benefit of the person using it for whatever purpose they are using it for.

Find Better Candidates, quickly

While at the workplace, we heavily depend upon machinery, humans are still the backbone of every business. Artificial intelligence will help identify things like for how long workers stay in a particular position, what's the cost per hire, which positions are quickly filled and which take longer. Company's process mining technology can help the businesses in understanding how their employees are behaving.

With the help of artificial intelligence in business, the human resources department can increase the efficiency in recruitment process and can reduce the costs by 30%. This will ultimately help in hiring the perfect candidate quickly.

Say No to Errors and Theft

We are all human, and we are bound to make errors. No matter how minor they are, errors do affect business. If the AI system is properly developed, artificial intelligence can eliminate the tiniest of human error and create an almost risk-free environment for the company.

For a company that is heavily dependent on internet, laptops, smartphones and other such devices, one of the biggest fear is a cyber-attack or theft. With the use of artificial intelligence, businesses can avoid these frauds and save themselves from massive losses because AI learns about the patterns, algorithms, system and decodes deviations, it can reveal in process-attacks and malfunctions.

Customer Service

Customer service is one of the most crucial aspects of any business. Customers are what make your business. It is one of the most time-consuming processes as well. A single complaint of customer issue can take hours to solve and you cannot make the blunder of either avoiding the mistake or not rectifying it fully. But with more customers explaining their problems through chat bots, the time taken to resolve a complaint can be cut short.

Although chat bots still lack that personal touch; with time, as the technology evolves, so will they. Apart from that, tools like Digital Genius are now used to create a flawless, human-like conversation with the customer.

With the help of artificial intelligence services, companies can collect more and more data, process it and get to know their consumers and their behavior patterns better. This will help in updating their services to satisfy their customers in a better way.

Measuring Big Data

Artificial intelligence companies won't be able to work without big data. With no data to work on, all the AI algorithms will be rendered useless. Big Data and AI are the two terms that are going to be the future of any business in the upcoming era and they complement one another. It is essential for a business to preserve the data generated in the vast amount, so they don't miss out on anything. Preserving the data is also important for making forecasts in future and to conduct fundamental analysis. Machines capable of performing evidence-based reasoning can speedup and improve decisions for a company dealing in people's management.

When it comes to managing big data, artificial intelligence and its algorithm-based branches like machine learning and deep learning are used to do it. It is used in finding trends, patterns, and predictions. Imagine how useful will it be especially for a stock market or finance business!

Lead Generation

Lead generation is the process of identifying and cultivating potential customers for a business's products or services. For any company, any expenses linked to consumer acquisition via lead generation are indispensable. Top AI companies are now using some AI systems that can process data better than the human brain can. These AI-based systems analyze consumer behavior from their social media and understand their interest and compiles a clear picture of buyer persona using this information.

There are a plenty of AI-based lead generation tools out there, the marketer needs to find out these tools and use it to their advantage. One such tool hiding in plain sight is LinkedIn's Sales Navigator tool. It hunts down the right leads on LinkedIn and helps you engage with them better. With the use of right kind of AI tools, you can even work to convert your leads to sales because sales are what you need. Getting leads to no fruition will take your business nowhere.

AI MARKETING

Artificial intelligence marketing is a method of leveraging customer data and AI concepts like machine learning to anticipate your customer's next move and improve the customer journey.

The evolution of big data and advanced analytic solutions has made it easier for marketers to build a clearer picture of their target audiences and in this opportunity of advancement lies AI marketing.

Armed with big data insights, marketers can greatly boost their campaigns' performance and ROI, all of which can be achieved with essentially no over the board effort on the marketer's part.

BENEFITS OF AI MARKETING

AI marketing has been gaining more attention of the marketers because of the insights it provides. Most of the big shots in the industry view AI marketing as a huge 'business advantage'.

More Intelligent Searches

As technology grows smarter, it's important to remember that audiences are becoming smarter as well. Thanks to social media and well developed search engines, people can find what they are looking for faster than ever before. AI and big data solutions can actually analyze these search patterns and guide the marketers to identify key areas where they should focus their efforts.

Smarter Ads

Marketers are already taking advantage of smarter ads, with account-based marketing solutions, but AI helps the marketing teams take this a notch up by providing a truly insightful analysis. With this abundance of data available, online ads can be made smarter, customized and more effective in generating leads and conversions. AI solutions can dig deeper into keyword searches, social profiles of potential customers, and other online data for aligning with human-level outcomes.

Refined Content Delivery

With AI, marketers can take data and targeting to a whole new level. Audience analytics can go past the typical demographics, to understand people on an individual basis. Now, marketers can use AI to both identify potential clients or buyers, and deliver ideally the content that's most relevant to them. With big data, machine learning, and AI combined, there is little an astute and intelligent marketer can't achieve.

Relying on Bots

Customer service and retention is another area where AI will play a huge role in the future. AI bots will soon run chat functions and other direct-to-consumer engagement avenues. AI bots also have access to an entire internet's worth of data, information, and search histories, making them much more efficient than their human counterparts so by deploying the AI bots for marketing, the marketers can save a lot of money and time that they'd spend on using manpower for the same.

Continued Learning

Not only can AI be used to uncover once-hidden insights, it can actually be taught to incorporate previously uncovered insights into new campaigns, optimizing outreach to target only the most relevant users. Over time, these AI solutions are destined to become even more intelligent, better at analyzing, efficient at targeting, greatly increasing conversions, and promoting real-time decision-making.

THE FUTURE OF ARTIFICAL INTELLIGENCE

AI marketing is not a bubble dream. It is real and is only bound to become bigger and better in the future. The future belongs to AI marketing; with many businesses switching to AI powered security, data analysis, data retention, insights and document processing.

It speeds up and improves the core processors of a business. Whether a business uses the AI or not, it will be greatly affected by it:

COMPETITORS ARE ALREADY USING AI

Almost 60% of businesses have already implemented AI based technologies in their business activities. Even if you aren't using AI to make your operations more efficient and to reduce costs, you will still be affected. Why? Because your competitor is using it to improve their sales and the overall operations. You're likely falling behind.

AI IS NOW A PART OF EVERY SEGMENT OF BUSINESS TECHNOLOGY

Artificial intelligence, paired with machine learning algorithms, is being introduced to all sectors of business technology. Businesses are all incorporating AI for their automation and analysis.

With the help of security suites, the businesses can use AI technology to identify the behavior of potentially malicious programs. This is especially important for the concerns of cyber security.

Facial Recognition can also be used for security purposes. Biometric devices installed outside offices assure that only those people who are familiar can enter into the premises where your valuable work is being carried out.

Human brain is extremely intelligent but it cannot process the huge amounts of data because we can't use our brain to full potential. AI facilitates data analysis and pattern matching of big data and streamlines the business operations more smoothly.

What is one going to do with collecting all this data and just shoving it into the memory of the computer. The data is modeled and stimulated to forecast the favorable outcomes in order to plan and conduct the future business activities accordingly.

AI is proliferating so quickly across all spectrums of business and takes the place of human workers; every time AI is implemented, it reduces costs.

As your business begins to implement AI, your business will find that all of its operations are faster and less costly. Businesses implementing AI should see a marked decline in their overhead costs and may even be able to reduce the size of their physical offices.

However, the major ways artificial intelligence may impact your business will stem from your company's unique operations and needs. It's not always easy to find the best ways to integrate new and advanced technologies into your existing work operations but in order to not fall behind your competition, you need to.

DO OR DIE CO-FOUNDER

To be an entrepreneur is one of the best decisions you will ever make in your life but amongst the many factors that go behind the execution of this decision, one of the most important questions is, "Should you start your venture alone?" Some people decide to take their dream by the lapels alone while others take it important to have someone stand alongside them throughout this life-changing journey and to build the company that is now a responsibility and an asset for both of you.

WHY CAN HAVING A CO-FOUNDER BE HELPFUL?

Moral support

Founding a business and running it is no easy journey. There will be days when you will be stressed and under extreme pressure of work. There will also be days when you start losing hope and think about giving up. No one will understand your situation better than a co-founder. Associates, juniors and friends may empathize with you but they will never quite understand your position since they cannot put themselves in your shoes.

Getting through the mental blocks

When your brain jams and you see no solution, that's when you really need a partner. Brainstorming sessions help you grow, bond better with your co-founder and come up with creative solutions. You can discuss your ideas and have the other person analyze it and modify it given any loopholes. These discussions form the backbone of any startup.

Investor support

It is not a secret that a considerable amount of investment goes into any startup. Investors rarely support single founders because they trust teams and multiple founders easily and feel more comfortable to fund such startups. So unless you already have millions kept aside to facilitate funding, you'll have to have a co-founder to ease the funding process.

Affirming decisions

When making solo decisions, you wouldn't be able to decide what is right and what is wrong. When there are more people to talk it out with, you'll know how good or bad your ideas are. Your friends and family will stick to just advising you or just agree with you to keep your spirits high. Only a co-founder can help in making decisions.

Get some rest

As a single founder, you'll hardly get a moment to breathe. If you fall ill, no one else can really take your place. It's only human to fall sick, your business needs you to show up every single day. A co-founder will be able to stand in for your absence and this can also give you your much-needed rest. Sometimes there will be important meetings and in case due to unfavorable circumstances you are not able to show up, your co-founder can handle the situation.

This way, both of you will have each other's backs all the time, in both good and bad times.

Equal profits and losses

Yes, you divide your profits with your co-founder, but do not forget that the burden of losses gets equally distributed, too. It is not possible for one person to have all the money to invest. Having a partner might take this problem out of the question.

Balance of skill

A business requires more than just an idea – it requires different skill sets, right from marketing to accounts, coding, website designing, and talking to clients. One person cannot embody all these skills. It's almost next to impossible for one person to handle everything to perfection. This is where the partner steps in, allowing the work to flow smoothly. You could divide departments according to your skill set as well as that of your co-founder's and combine those efforts to the benefit of your business.

A helping hand

Starting a business is hard. The reason why many people choose to stick to corporate jobs is because they are comfortable. They do not want to step out of their comfort zones and take risks. there is a fixed schedule and you have a lot of time at your hands.

However, we have discussed enough the benefits of being self-employed. They are the brave ones who take a step towards making their dream true. But they do realize that it is no cakewalk. To sail smoothly through this hard process, having a partner is important and none better than a co-founder who shares the good, the bad and the ugly with you.

THE RIGHT CO-FOUNDER?

Imagine what would happen if you were married to a person you are not compatible with? Wouldn't your life become a living hell?

A business is no less important than a marriage and your business partner needs to be at least as compatible with you, if not more, as you would want your life partner to be.

SKILLS THAT COMPLEMENT YOURS: You wouldn't want your co-founder to be a replica of you. You would want them to have skills that are different yet complementary to yours. For example: If you are an extrovert, they should be an introvert.

VISIONS THAT ALIGN: If you are an extremely ambitious person, you wouldn't want to share the reins of your business with someone who is lazy. Their objectives and attitudes must fall in line with yours for your venture to be successful. You both must possess the same goal and want to achieve the same thing.

EMOTIONAL INTELLIGENCE AND ENERGY: A person who cannot tackle his emotions becomes vulnerable and vulnerable is the last thing a person must be in order to be successful in business. A person must also always be excited and enthusiastic in doing the daunting tasks to keep your business running uphill. You need to be this person and your co-founder must possess these qualities too.

ADAPTABLE AND FLEXIBLE: An entrepreneur has to perform a variety of tasks throughout the day. Your co-founder must be someone who can easily adapt with the different hats they'll need to wear along with you. They must have an attitude of grit.

HONESTY AND TRANSPERANCY: There's a lot you put at risk when you decide to co-find business with someone. You must build an initial level of trust but remember to be legally secure and sound before getting into this relationship with anyone.

DIGITAL MARKETING TOOLS THAT A BUSINESS DEVELOPER MUST KNOW.

Tools of the trade are the ride or die of any trade. No matter the size of the enterprise, the deployment of the tools of digital marketing are indispensable and are always utilized to the good of the company. Irrespective of the task that is assigned digital marketing tools come in handy when completing those successfully. The tools also serve to save time and mitigate the work pressure to some extent.

The following are a few tools that exist in the Digital Marketing Universe to make the job easier every day:

SPROUT SOCIAL:

Sprout social enables top-notch engagement, optimization, publishing, analytics and team collaboration tools. Social sprout is a social media management platform for businesses. Sprout is a powerful platform for social businesses available via web browser, iOS and android that enables brands to more effectively communicate across social channels, collaborate across teams and provides a fine customer experience.

Social sprout is an intuitive platform and was created with the user in mind, making it easy for the user to publish content on a schedule, scheduled prior to the posting time.

Social sprout makes it easy for the user to publish content across various social media channels, monitor their social presence, engage with their audience and analyze social media efforts across all connected profiles. It can be exhausting to manage multiple social media websites together and to keep up with the time of posting. Social Sprout helps solve this problem and serves as a bridge between you and your social media accounts.

You can schedule a post on sprout social and link it to whatever social media portals you wish for that post to appear on. Sprout Social will automatically send the post on those social media portals. It is a very effective tool to save time.

WYNG:

Wyng was formerly known as Offerpop. It is an engagement generating platform which focuses on garnering engagement on the user generated content, hashtags, campaigns, referral programs, quizzes, contests and more.

What good will good content anyway be if it does not get good attention. The content will go waste and so it is very important to generate substantial engagement on it. Wyng is a platform designed to do just that.

Marketing effectiveness is now increasingly driven by consumer influence and brands have a new potential to activate and unite customers. This calls for a need for an active engagement with customers. Keeping pace with technology and innovation, Wyng has come quite far while also helping the brands to grow and evolve. Wyng works to elevate their customer influence by providing a marketing platform for brands and companies to build and run campaigns that drive participation.

WOOBOX:

Similar to Wyng, Woobox is a social engagement platform that emphasizes on increasing the interactivity of the content. The platform is perhaps best known as a turnkey solution for running social giveaways and competitions, Instagram contests in particular. From curating hashtag entries to selecting winners at random, WooBox takes much of the hard work out of running any kind of contest or giveaway on social media.

It allows you to run sweepstakes, contests, polls, and more across Facebook, Twitter, Google+, YouTube, LinkedIn, Pinterest and Vine.

Woobox is a tool to help brands and companies grow their social followings and create a buzz around their products. It's an ideal tool for eCommerce brands that want to increase immediate engagement and interest in their products.

Woobox allows you to streamline your Facebook advertising by promoting your offer or post, manage your audiences, set up custom ad triggers, and remarket them to users that have already visited your website. You can also set up a Facebook Page Tab for the contests. You can then easily track the performance of your contest in the Woobox interface.

Woobox also offers various kinds of offers for you to choose from, you can choose an offer which deems fit to your needs. Creating a Woobox offer is really simple, once you know what kind of offer you want to run. The following are all the available offer types you can choose from:

Coupon: You can create fan-only coupons with unique coupon codes.

Sweepstakes: You can collect any number entries over a certain period of time, and then pick one or more winners for your grand prize.

Pinterest PintoWin: Users must pin to Pinterest for a chance to win your offer.

Instant Win: You can set the odds of winning to whatever you gauge, allowing users a chance of winning a prize straight away. This is different from a Sweepstakes because you don't have to pick the winner yourself; they are chosen automatically.

Photo Contest: You can create photo contests that let fans submit photos and vote for their favorites too.

Video Contest: You can create video contests that let fans submit videos and vote for their favorites; which is very similar to the photo contest.

UGC Contest: You can also create a user-generated content (UGC) content that lets fans submit their original content and then vote for their favorite.

Poll: You can create questions to gain feedback from your followers which you further use to frame your policies.

Quiz: You can create quizzes with custom results which will help to increase the interactivity of the content.

Group Deal: This option will create coupons that are only available, as the name "group deal" suggests, after a certain number of people request the coupon.

Deal: This requires payment via PayPal to access the offer.

Reward: This allows you to create rewards that can only be accessed by people that are on your guest list. This is in simple words some kind of a VIP option.

Leaderboard Contest: You can collect entries for leaderboard contests and display the results and standings as the entries process advances.

Bracket: This option lets users create brackets, score them, and then displays leaderboards as it advances.

Landing Page: This allows you to create a landing page offer.

Form: This option makes you create a form submission offer.

Download App: This allows you to create an app offer which are getting more popular each day.

After selecting the type of offer you wish to create, Woobox guides you step by step through adding all the details.

Woobox is one of the best organic tools that you can use in your business development and digital marketing practice to expand and grow business by making the most out of the created content.

NANIGANS:

A major tool of choice for companies such as Zynga, Wayfair and Rovio, Nanigans is a multichannel advertising software with an emphasis specifically on Facebook marketing. Its software has access to the Facebook Exchange (FBX) for retargeting and also a large number of other tools that make targeting more efficient. Beyond Facebook remarketing, the platform also has features focused around Twitter ads and Instagram growth as well.

Nanigans has been revolutionising how marketers acquire and remarket to customers. By making the best use of the power of lifetime value to inform more intelligent and efficient media buying, the company is moving the industry away from buying on a cost-per-click and cost-per-action basis to a lifetime ROI basis. Furthermore, Nanigans' Ad Engine is the only advertising platform that measures, predicts and optimizes ad spend for lifetime ROI on both interfaces, the desktop and the mobile. Chosen by the world's leading and most efficient marketers in sectors such as retail and gaming, Ad Engine delivers over 2 billion Facebook ad impressions every day that drive over 2 million daily conversions into purchases.

Nanigans was founded in 2010 as an early Facebook Ads API developer and was recently designated by Facebook a Strategic Preferred Marketing Developer (sPMD). Backed by Avalon Ventures and with offices in Boston, New York, San Francisco and London, Nanigans is growing rapidly with the winning advantage of today's most competitive performance advertisers.

With a decade of experience in successfully challenging and tackling ad industry norms, Nanigans offers marketing teams unmatched strategic guidance and radical control through a tried and tested ad management platform.

As partners to CMOs and in-house marketers around the world, Nanigans powers an ownable competitive advantage that delivers the performance growing businesses need to win.

FACEBOOK'S POWER EDITOR:

The Power Editor is Facebook's own tool for creating and running hyper-specific advertising campaigns. Facebook is constantly improving its ad platform, and the tool releases new targeting and budgeting features for users. For marketers who are just starting on the paid social front, this is without any doubt one of the best digital marketing tools with no middlemen fee to create and manage your advertisements. The platform's detailed parameters ensure that you target exactly who you want and not keep running around in circles; meanwhile, you can also set limits to avoid exhausting or going overboard with your budget.

If you want a more precise control of your Facebook ads or access to advanced Facebook features not available in the Facebook Ads Manager, Power Editor is your answer.

Power Editor offers advanced features that can help you reach your perfect audience with the right message.

Power Editor is a bulk ads creation and management tool typically used by larger Facebook advertisers or advertisers who want to work with advanced features. Power Editor is essentially a plugin that works with Google Chrome and works on a download and upload system, so every time you want to work in Power Editor you download all of your data from the Ads Manager and then create your campaigns, ads and ad sets that are provided within Power Editor.

Power Editor has a lot more interesting features. One benefit is that typically new features are added here first before they are launched to the Ads Manager area, so you have early access to all of the newest features.

The following are a few benefits of the Facebook power editor:
- If you know your audience is only on Facebook at certain times of day, you can make the most of your ad performance by showing your ads at those local times; which makes the advertising time zone independent. This will lead to more interactive activity.
- If you're an app developer, controlling the placement of your ads can be very useful because you can **advertise to the people on the right cellular phone.** You can also choose to only **show your ad to cellular phone when they're connected to WiFi.**

- In Power Editor you can optimize your ad for the same things available in the Ads Manager such as clicks, post engagement for when you're doing a boosted post ad or impressions.

- If you're running a lot of ads, you may be interested in the bulk uploading feature. It allows you to **upload an Excel spreadsheet of your ads** and download them too, if and when you need to edit them.

- One of the most prominent reasons to use Power Editor is the Unpublished Post option. An unpublished post looks similar to a regular page post in that it has longer text, but it also includes a call-to-action button and you can control what the link looks like per your liking.

TWITTER NATIVE PLATFORM:

Twitter is another major network brands should consider paying to advertise on. Twitter has some incredible features for targeting, with functionality that includes the ability to target certain keywords so that whenever someone Tweets out, or engages with a Tweet, using that key phrase they'll be automatically targeted. The platform is especially useful when targeting mobile users, as 86% of Twitter's ad revenue came just from mobile in 2015.

With over 300 million monthly active users and a young demographic to boot, Twitter is a great platform for many marketers.

Starting up a Twitter page for your company is very easy. Anyone can come up with a Twitter handle, upload their profile photo, fill out their bio and post their Tweets. What's not so simple, however, is growing your Twitter account and turning it into an actual tool that generates leads and builds up your brand that is to monetize it.

Growing a real following on Twitter takes more than sending out Tweets whenever your company has a product being released or an upcoming event. It's about engaging with your target audience and interacting with them. Successful Twitter marketing is extremely powerful. If you can become deft with this fast paced social networking site, you'll unlock new opportunities to grow your business online.

For years, marketers have wondered about getting more Twitter followers. But the question they should really be asking is "how to get more active Twitter followers?" The answer is Twitter chats. Twitter chats are a useful tool and it's nice to see a lot of marketers slowly start to realize the power of Twitter chats when it comes to gaining active followers.

The reason why Twitter chats are so effective is because the people who participate in them are the ones that enjoy actively engaging on the social network. They don't use it just to distribute and consume content from social media. Instead, these people use Twitter for the purpose it was meant for, which is to interact. These are the types of users who are going to reply to your Tweets, Retweet your content and hence amplify your message.

To get started, look for Twitter chats related to your industry. If you're in the marketing industry or target business owners and entrepreneurs, look for twitter chats around topics like content marketing, social media and business; you can always use Google as well.

Can't find any Twitter chats for your industry? Start your own. The key to success with Twitter chats is to be more than a spectator. You have to add value to the conversation in order to differentiate yourself. For example, create a special graphic instead of just Tweeting text? Tools like Canva make it extremely easy to create a beautiful Twitter image within a couple minutes.

Your approach to every social media site should be different. For example, your Twitter marketing strategy isn't going to be the same as your Pinterest or Facebook or Instagram marketing plan. Understanding how Twitter works and where it fits in the social media landscape will shape the way you use it.

Some of the principle ways in which businesses use Twitter include:

- Sharing information and content
- Driving engagement for promotional activities
- Interacting with consumers
- Networking
- Building brand presence

As is discussed, most of these activities have to do with interactions. It's not necessarily just about broadcasting your content like Instagram or Pinterest, for example. Twitter thrives off of communication. Keep that in mind as we continue with the rest of your marketing on twitter.

MAILCHIMP:

MailChimp represents a gargantuan giant within the email marketing space, with **over 250 billion emails sent** by its users. The beauty of MailChimp is the platform's usability and sliding price tag based on the size of your email list. In particular, their "forever free" plan is perfect for smaller marketers looking for an introduction to email marketing. For a person just getting acquainted with digital marketing tools or email in general, MailChimp represents a great starting point.

MailChimp is one of the biggest success stories in marketing software startups. Millions of people and businesses are now using the platform to send over a billion emails every day and MailChimp is the first name that comes to mind when many people think about email marketing.

MailChimp enables people interested in your work or products to subscribe and unsubscribe to email marketing lists through sign-up forms, which are mostly placed on a website's sidebar. Emails sent to the user's lists are called campaigns, which can be sent using reusable email designs called templates. Newsletters fall into MailChimp's "Regular Ol' Campaign" category whereas having your blog posts delivered to subscribers via email falls into the "RSS-Driven Campaign" category.

Initial registration consists of creating a username, password, and security questions. The user's name and physical address must be provided so MailChimp can automatically build email footers that comply with the spam laws. Your mailing address MUST appear at the bottom of the newsletter, so you might want to consider using a post office box. With self-hosted websites you will have to consider using the customized email address provided by your webhost.

The MailChimp Dashboard This is command central for creating lists, designing forms, and sending campaigns. At all stages in the process, MailChimp offers clickable links to information that will help guide you through the task at hand.

A list must be created before the user can send their first campaign or create a subscription form to place on their website. Email addresses can be manually added or imported, but people need to opt-in or subscribe to your list. That means you have sought their permission.

The marketer needs to take into consideration the email marketing etiquette and spam laws. For instance, if a contact has not given permission, but you feel they might be interested, send just one short email asking them to subscribe and be sure to provide a link to the form. Also be careful that if your account is flagged too often for spam, it can be suspended.

Visitors to your site need to sign-up for your newsletter or blog to receive your blog posts via email. First, build the form as needed. Then you need to write the body of the mail, and finally, you can share your sign-up form. MailChimp assigns the form its own URL to make it easy to share via Twitter and Facebook.

An another way to share the sign up form is the HTML link is provided for use within documents or in the sign-off section at the end of a blog post.

The final option allows the creation of an HTML code to create a small subscribtion form that can be placed in a blog's sidebar as a widget.

Once you've created at least one list and its sign-up form, you can start working on your first campaign.

Pick a name for your campaign. Also pick a subject line of your email. MailChimp offers a subject line researcher which will indicate the open-rate for various subjects, but you have to allow pop-ups on your computer.

Design the look of your campaign. Pick a template and start playing around with the format. Most are mobile-friendly versions and preview and hence test email modes can be entered as needed. Plenty of sample newsletters are also available to help you get new and creative ideas.

EMMA:

Emma, the name is derived as an abbreviation for email marketing is a robust platform that backs up its powerful features with an extremely efficient hands-on customer service team. Emma has all of the tools that you can think you need to start creating and testing your own email marketing campaigns.

Emma is a cloud-based email marketing platform that helps users design email campaigns and also review their performance. The solution can be, using native applications used on multiple devices, including smartphones and tablets.

Emma helps marketing teams design email programs, segment audiences based on demographics, tenure or spending history and send automated emails. It also helps users track performance metrics for individual emails or for the entire program and provide insights using dashboards and reports. Emma also lets users deliver follow-up emails by providing an analysis about if the recipient had opened the email or clicked the link sent to them.

Emma is built to help users understand which content performs well by analyzing emails with the best click-through rates. Other features included are drag-and-drop editor, customizable templates, open API and integration with other applications, such as Salesforce, SurveyMonkey, Shopify, Wistia and Front Desk.

Emma offers various differentially-priced editions that are targeted to suit to different user segments, including universities, agencies, franchises and nonprofit organizations.

MARKETO:

If you've already played around with some email platforms and wish to take it to an advanced level, Marketo could be what you are looking for. Although email is a huge part of its business, it is not the only part of the tool. This makes Marketo ideal for those who are in search of all "all-in-one" weapon for their marketing. Marketo takes automation as a part of its array of digital marketing tools, with email marketing as a major part of it.

Marketo is a Software-as-a-Service (SaaS) marketing automation platform designed to automate the process of engaging with prospective and existing customers through digital channels. Systems like Marketo are important to the modern B2B marketer because B2B buyers are extremely self-directed and control their buying cycle more than vendors control the selling cycle.

Marketo is SaaS based marketing automation software built to help organizations automate and measure marketing engagement and tasks. Mareto sells marketing automation software to help B2B and B2C marketers target qualified leads, produce lead-to-revenue opportunities and execute automated, personalized marketing campaigns across multiple digital channels.

Per the Salesforce State of Marketing Report, more than 67 percent of marketing leaders currently use a marketing automation platform. The question that arises is who typically uses Marketo's software? Mareto users belong to three different arrays:

- Marketing practitioners who require getting campaigns built and strategies operationalized.
- Sales reps who have insight into all the digital behavior of their prospective clients and can now have a better and more contextual engagement
- Marketing executives who can now correlate marketing investment to sales and revenue.

Ryan Vong, president and CEO of Marketo partner Digital Pi, said that, Marketo users may be in demand generation, marketing operations, sales, executives, sales and marketing agencies, product management, product marketing, brand managers and marketing administrators. Irrespective of the company size, business and maturity almost anyone can be a Marketo user. "The ways in which companies can and do use Marketo is quite large, and very diverse, which implies that there is a variety of users that use Mareto.

GETRESPONSE:

GetResponse's unique email marketing platform works upon the growing trend of automation. This solution analyzes specific trends and behaviors from your email list to trigger specific messages and auto responders right away. The result of this is a better email marketing presence and a more engaged list.

Getresponse is an email marketing app that facilitates you with creating a mailing list, capturing data in the list, creating newsletters to be sent to the subscribers on your mailing list, automating your emails to subscribers via 'autoresponders', viewing and analyzing statistics related to your email marketing campaigns which are open rate, click through, forwards etc.

Getresponse's feature set has been evolving remarkably, and now it has become a more of an 'all-in-one' marketing platform.

In addition to email marketing, it also provides services like webinar hosting, landing pages, automated sales funnels and CRM (customer relationship management) serviceability.

Getresponse has been around since 1998; and, per the statistics, more than 400,000 individuals and businesses now use the platform for their email marketing.

Not only does Getresponse provide all the core tools expected from an email marketing platform viz list hosting, templates, autoresponders, analytics to name a few, but it's recently been expanding its feature set to the point where it has developed into an all-in-one marketing and e-commerce platform.

Getresponse represents one of the most economic ways to host and communicate with your email database, it is also competitively priced in the marketplace.

It's also one of the more interesting products of its kind because it provides email marketing, automation, landing pages, e-commerce, sales funnels, some CRM functionality and webinars all in a single space.

It's hard to think of any other product currently existing that offers this 'all rounder' status, and it's what continues to persuade brands to use Getresponse as a medium for their email marketing.

Pros of using Getresponse

- It gives you excellent marketing automation options.
- So long as you are happy to use a 'Basic' plan, Getresponse is cheaper than many of its key competitors but offers just as much, if not more functionality as them.
- The discounts you receive when paying upfront for one or two years of service are indeed incredible, it'll be tough to find similar discounts from key competitors.
- The 'Autofunnel' feature is potentially useful for merchants who want to manage all aspects of their sales funnels and e-commerce activity in a single place.
- Its webinar functionality is it's USP. It is something that is not offered by any similar products.
- Similarly, the CRM functionality is fairly unique amongst competing products.
- The reporting and comprehensive split testing features are quite strong.

- Getresponse is transparent about deliverability rates, publishing figures on its website and providing deliverability statistics for the e-newsletters that you send out.
- It offers a good approach to data segmentation, it's far more flexible on this front than many competing products.
- It sends responsive emails and allows you to preview smartphone versions of your e-newsletters easily.
- All Getresponse plans come with a useful landing page creator that facilitates A/B testing which is something that could potentially save you a lot of money.
- Custom DKIM (Domain Keys Identified Mail) is provided on all plans.
- It provides good tools for complying with GDPR (General Data Protection Regulation).
- 24/7 support is included on all plans.

ADROLL:

AdRoll is one of the most popular names in the retargeting space, boasting of a customer base of over 35,000 advertisers. This platform grants access to over 500 ad exchanges, which includes most of the major social media networks. It offers a self-service platform, but you can also leverage its employees for any additional help if needed. The success stories behind many AdRoll users are absolutely insane, with reports ranging from a 35% lower CPC to a drastic %265 lift in sales in a few cases.

AdRoll is the global leader in retargeting with many thousand active advertisers worldwide. The AdRoll platform helps businesses in a wide range of industries, uses their customer data to execute high-performance campaigns across platforms and devices that attract and convert prospects into customers.

Campaign Monitor users can easily sync their subscriber lists to AdRoll to target in their display campaigns. AdRoll offers substantial degree of transparency and reach across the largest ad sources on the web and social. The company also introduced AdRoll Prospecting to attract new customers to help advertisers reach beyond their existing audiences.

AdRoll's LiquidAds help to create dynamic, personalised ads that boost the retargeting performance.

RETARGETER:

ReTargeter is a diverse tool that uses site retargeting, search retargeting and dynamic retargeting. You can use ReTargeter as a self-service platform or for another option you can pass all of your campaigns onto an account team to run the retargeting operation for you. You can use these search services separately or combine several into a custom package. The platform emphasizes use for ecommerce brands with a condition that the ReTargeter must have access to consumer behavioral data of over 150 of the web's top retailers.

Retargeting, also known as remarketing, is a form of online advertising that can help you keep your brand in front of traffic even after they leave your website. For most websites, only 2% of web traffic converts on the first visit. Retargeting is a tool designed to help companies reach the 98% of users who don't convert right away and hence convert a few more prospects into customers.

Retargeting as a technology is cookie-based and uses simple Javascript code to anonymously follow your audience all over the Web.

This is how it works: you place a small, demure piece of code on your website, or a pixel on your website. The code, or pixel, is unnoticeable to your site visitors and won't affect your site's performance in any manner. Every time a new visitor comes to your site, the code drops an anonymous browser cookie. Later, when your cookied visitors browse the Web, irrespective of what they are doing, the cookie will let your retargeting provider know when to serve ads, ensuring that your ads are served to only to people who have already previously visited your site.

Retargeting is so effective because it focuses your advertising spend on people who are already familiar with your brand and have also demonstrated interest. That's why most marketers who use it see a higher ROI than from most other digital marketers who do not.

CHOICESTREAM:

ChoiceStream's technology is able to process a ton of audience data and distinguish which of it is actually useful knowledge for brands.

ChoiceStream then uses that information to properly target ads to your audiences which it knows to be a good fit, boosting the relevance of your ads to your targets.

ChoiceStream is the main media organization that accepts crowd's sections by asking individuals what they like, what they need and what they think. They make inquiries at Pollshare.com, which is a shopper site owned by and worked upon by ChoiceStream, and utilize the experiences they assemble to collect the information that comes in with each promotion call.

ChoiceStream is a data driven ad platform that runs cross-gadget branding and direct reaction crusades for brand and office customers. ChoiceStream deals with every period of a campaign, from pre-dispatch wanting to fulfillment.

ROCKETFUEL:

Rocket Fuel is a popular tool with a feature called "Moment Scoring" which sets it apart from any competition. Moment Scoring assesses anonymous user data to calculate how likely someone is to respond to your advertisement and then uses that information to evaluate the time and place to serve your ads. Rocket Fuel offers both, a self-service platform and managed services platform.

Retailers use big data in many ways to ensure they are delivering the best customer service and experience and to ultimately boost the business performance. Loyalty programs capture data that gives an understanding of what a customer purchases regularly and patterns of their purchase behaviour. Point-of-sale data determines when customers are shopping and if they are taking advantage of deals and sales. And overall sales figures can point towards whether an advertising campaign is having the desired effect. All of this quantitative data can be combined to help retailers make important and effective qualitative business decisions.

But it is not just about using this data to change future marketing strategies or assess previous performance, it is now possible to take all of this data and turn it into strategies for growth, retention and scaling businesses in real time. A programmatic solution has access to so much data – purchase behaviour, demographics, psychographics, geographic data and so on. It can make crucial decisions on which customer should be targeted with which product in a matter of seconds. Some companies can access data segments from multiple third-party data providers, as well as retailers' owned first-hand data, allowing for the creation of custom audiences, whether you are looking to retarget previous shoppers or preparing a prospect for brand new customers.

Retailers have lalways known the benefits of retargeting and many are revisiting their strategies to make sure they are getting the best. This means leveraging data on what a consumer is in the market for, targeting them with a reason for purchasing and then tying that back to their purchase data to cease marketing to that customer the purchased product and now advertise the related products. This leads to either marketing to that consumer or looking at cluster analysis of purchases or buying behaviour to cross-sell other products. All this can be automated and provides increased revenue opportunities and that too at lower costs.

SIMPLI.FI:

Simpli.fi differentiates itself from other tools by taking complete advantage of an unstructured audience data. This means that unlike some other tools on the market—Simpli.fi doesn't rely on pre-made audience segments to categorize audience data. This is a huge advantage when working with a lot of data.

Local programmatic platform Simpli.fi is creating Conversion Zones to sharpen the boundaries of its geofences as part of the company's work to prove that the ads it serves not only reaches the desired consumer target, but also that those location-based marketing strategies also drives consumers into a store.

Conversion Zones are customizable geofences around a set area that counts the number of consumers that have received a place's mobile ad and could be tracked physically to mark that they visited a location. Great! Isn't it? The promise of Conversion Zones, like other forms of attribution, is meant to provide the advertisers with a clear view of how effective their geo-targeted ads are along consumers' path to purchase.

Simpli.fi's offering comes amid a plethora of other online-to-offline attribution products entering the mobile and cross-device marketplace.

UNBOUNCE:

Unbounce is an amazing tool for quickly building, tweaking and publishing new landing pages to test. One of the most fantastic features of Unbounce is how easy it is to use the platform to create absolutely new pages. Even if you're not much of a designer, you can use some of the templates available as a starting point, then edit them to fit your style.

Unbounce is used by marketing teams and agencies to create landing pages which are custom pages dedicated to a single campaign or a conversion goal as opposed to sending traffic to the homepage or elsewhere and overlays which are targeted calls-to-action that can appear on top of any web page, without having to depend upon the designers or developers.

It's designed to empower marketers with the deftness, speed and customization they need to launch and loop campaigns for maximum conversions. A/B testing, drag-and-drop functionality, lead generation, CRM integration, a rich mobile-responsive template gallery and dynamic text replacement for better AdWords Quality Score are some of the features that help Unbounce keep up with this promise.

ORACLE MAXYMISER:

Maxymiser is a tool that goes far beyond the realm of landing page testing. This enterprise-level software solution was built to test multiple aspects of any given site and to run several different tests at once. Maxymiser also allows you to segment who you want to send to each test, creating a more systematic experience for your website visitors.

With Oracle Maxymiser, marketers can optimize every part of the online and mobile app customer experience including website homepages, campaign landing pages, and multistep checkout funnels. It helps convert more visitors into customers, increase engagement and revenue and persuade them to keep coming back for more.

OPTIMIZELY:

Optimizely combines tools for visual creation and robust targeting into its platform, making it easy to quickly create and target tests to the proper groups of users. The company also has a good amount of partners that makes it easier to centralize customer data for your various tests.

Optimizely is an incredible optimization tool, but exactly how it works can be a little tricky until you go about exploring the mechanics.

If you don't have a strong technical background, your eyes might not understand anything when you hear something like "Optimizely allows you to perform A/B and multivariate testing using client-side JavaScript variation code so that you can compare different versions of an experience to determine which leads to a better user experience and more conversions."

The Optimizely snippet gets added to the source code of a webpage. There the snippet will stay until it's called into service. If no experiment is running, the snippet doesn't do anything; it just stays in the webpage and waits. If an experiment *is* running, then the algorithm will work.

Once the snippet is set up and a test is configured, nothing happens until a user requests the page. If the various targeting conditions are met the user will either be grouped into the "test" group or the "control" group.

The page starts to load and, if Optimizely is implemented correctly, the snippet will load quickly after it. The snippet springs into action as the page is loading. It doesn't *stop* the page from loading; it works along *as* the page is loading. If the user is in the "test" group, the snippet works its magic and changes the HTML on the fly using jQuery which is a more developed version of JavaScript. The Optimizely snippets rewrites the page as necessary before it finishes loading.

VISUAL WEBSITE OPTIMISER:

Even though the mantra of "always be testing" has become a bit cliché, there's no denying the importance of A/B testing any given page of your site. Visual Website Optimizer streamlines the process by allowing you to quickly tackle with elements of your pages such as headlines and images to generate multiple versions of your site for visitors to land on. Combined with a powerful analytics platform, you can quickly see which version of your site is running ahead in terms of clicks and conversions.

Visual Website Optimizer is a market leading testing and optimization tool that allows marketers, product managers and analysts to create A/B tests and geo-behavioral targeting campaigns even without having any sort of technical or HTML knowledge.

Visual Website Optimizer is an easy to use A/B testing tool that allows marketing professionals to create different versions of their websites and landing pages using a point-and-click editor which again requires no HTML knowledge and then see which version produces maximum conversion rate or sales.

Integration with Google Analytics allows you to create different versions of your webpage in VWO, and then do analysis of an A/B test in Google Analytics. Visual Web Site Optimizer is also a flexible multivariate testing software and has number of additional tools like behavioral targeting, heat maps, usability testing, etc. With more than a hundred features in Visual Website Optimizer, you can be sure that all your conversion rate optimization activities are covered by our product. Thousands of enterprises and small businesses are using Visual Website Optimizer for landing page optimization, increasing website sales and improving conversion rates.

HOTJAR:

Hot jar's platform provides a real-time visual record of your visitors' actions and behaviors on-site. Through heatmaps that clue you in on where people are or aren't clicking. It also provides actual video recordings of your visitor's journey, you can quite literally see what needs to be optimized rather than second-guess.

Hotjar is a powerful tool that provides an analysis of the online behavior and voice of your users. By combining both Analysis and Feedback tools, Hotjar gives you the 'big picture' of how to improve your site's user experience and performance and conversion rates.

The Analysis tools allow you to measure and observe user behavior while the Feedback tools enable you to "hear" what your users have to say.

Hotjar is **not** an alternative to Google Analytics. In fact, Hotjar should ideally be used together with a web analytics solution.

While web analytics software tools like Google Analytics will give you data about the pages your users are visiting. For instance, which page has the highest bounce rate or conversion rate, but they will not show you how your visitors are really using the pages themselves.

With Hotjar, you can understand your web and mobile site visitors by seeing how they interact with your pages and by understanding why they behave the way they do. This allows you to quickly identify opportunities for improvement and growth.

WISTIA:

The platform is amazing for brands looking to host, customize and share videos across the web. One of the best functions of its platform is the ability to include a custom CTA at the end of each individual video, making it easy to drive viewers to specific pages that you want.

If viewers share your video on YouTube rather than your home page or sales page, you are seriously missing out on the advantage that link provides. Instead, YouTube is getting all the traffic and revenue for themselves by serving up ads. That viewer will never see your site. You won't get that sale or signup. It's gone, and gone forever.

What good is a "sales video" without a call to action? Wistia gives you the ability to include a clickable call to action at the end of your video. Using this feature, you can drive more traffic to your sales page or wherever else you'd like to take your viewer. Much like the "Call to action", you can enable the video player to require someone to enter their email address before, in the middle or at the end of the video; wherever you may wish. They've even got it setup to integrate directly with your newsletter service providers.

Wistia Videos analytics gives amazing insights about how your videos are doing. There's an engagement graph that shows how engaged your viewers are at all times during the video as well as heat maps to see individual viewer insights and even a summary of loads, visitors, play rate, plays, hours watched and average engagement percentage.

Wistia was and continues to be built with web marketing in mind. It has video SEO tools built-in, allowing you to easily even if you are technically challenged, add metadata like Title, Description, Tags, Etc. so that your video comes up first in Google search results. They even make it easy for you to update your webpage's sitemap so Google's spider can easily find your videos for indexing.

VIMEO:

There are over 35 million people and businesses that trust Vimeo to host their high-definition, ad-free videos. With Vimeo, the concept is to get everyone to host some of their high-quality videos on the site, thereby driving viewers who are looking for visually stunning videos.

In 2017, Vimeo made a major strategic shift from being a destination where people came to watch high-end videos, to a software provider for video makers of all sizes and types. Vimeo's focus is capturing a larger share of a $20 billion market for video hosting, distribution and monetization. And this means being useful for a customer base that can include every type of video producer on the face of earth, from a social media star or media company publishing to various social platforms, to a yoga teacher streaming live video. Absolutely anything that you can think of!

Looking ahead, Vimeo sees growth opportunities with video makers interested in launching subscription services. Beyond its core software product for video makers, Vimeo also offers an OTT product that allows customers to spin up subscription streaming channels. That product is being used by more than 1,000 OTT subscription services, according to the company's analysis.

Vimeo's efforts to get in front of more publishers, marketers and other business owners have included an ad campaign featuring some impudent placements promoting what Vimeo can and can't do for video creators.

CANVA:

Canva is a free, web-based design tool you can use to create unique images to share on your blogs, social networks and beyond. You can use Canva to create completely unique images from scratch or to polish up some photos that you already have created.

Canva is an easy-to-use graphic design tool that you use right in your browser. It allows you to make professional-looking images and graphics and offers tons and tons of free and cheap services. You can start with common templates for your social media profiles, common post types, print documents and even Kindle book covers.

After creating your image, you can download your work as image files or PDFs. You can also immediately share them on your social media networks.

Canva is a tool loaded with enough easy-to-use features and functionality that anyone can create a variety of engaging content that gets shared. Canva really offers a variety of content types. From pre-sized social media image and header templates to marketing materials, documents, presentations, invitations and ads, you'll find almost everything you need.

Canva offers drag-and-drop functionality. Combined with search, this feature makes it easy to discover image elements and to include the ones you like.

Whether you use a free or paid photo, or even one you upload yourself, Canva provides and easy-to-use and user friendly photo editor where you can change the look of your image using settings that include filters, tint, brightness, and more.

LANDSCAPE BY SPROUT SOCIAL:

A great way to make sure your online content stands out is to include an image, but sourcing images that satisfy the unique requirements for each social network can be tough. The company solved this problem by coming up with this tool that quickly turns one image into multiple, each perfectly sized for the social media networks you're using.

It is a free tool that allows streamlined image resizing across the various social networks.

With so many different social networks commanding different ideal image sizes, the company found a need for an all-in-one solution that makes managing images across these various social networks a bit easier. Since these networks are forever changing, and the ideal image sizes, too, have needed to be changed on the basis of the evolution of the various sites images are posted to, the company felt it was necessary to keep marketers on the same side of the game.

FEEDLY:

With Feedly you can choose all of the different blogs, publications and topics that you're interested in; meanwhile, the platform aggregates all of the recent content from those sites into a feed that you can easily monitor. You can integrate your Feedly feed with a tool like Sprout Social to continuously share these articles with your fans and followers.

Feedly is a robust feed reader that aggregates information from around the web into one place. You can use it to view updates on any topic you›re interested in, whether they come from the news, blogs, social media posts, RSS feeds, or other sources.

The primary benefit of a feed reader like Feedly is that you get to see all of this information in one single place rather than having to separately visit each website, blog, etc., to get updates. You can use Feedly from your computer, the web, or your mobile device

Feedly aggregates, or collects, RSS feeds. An RSS feed provides a method for websites to publish information once and syndicate it automatically amongst millions of subscribers. An aggregator captures, and organizes, feeds to simplify the dissemination of news. No longer do we need to constantly revisit the same site, wondering what's new. Now we only need to add RSS feeds to our reader, also known as aggregators, and wait for the news to come to us. Readers provide information consumers with huge advantages.

Feedly possesses three advantages over most other RSS aggregation services. First, it has its own hosting service, meaning Feedly stores RSS feeds on its own servers. Earlier Google hosted RSS feeds and provided an API key to developers interested in creating mobile applications reliant on Google's servers as a support. When Reader died, so did the hosting service that virtually all RSS readers depended upon. Fortunately, Feedly stepped in and offered to pick up Google's weakness, preventing a mass dying off of RSS aggregators and other services.

SCOOP.IT:

Scoop.it is an awesome tool for easily finding and sharing unique, relevant content to your social networks, blogs and more. With Scoop.it you can find months' worth of information in no time flat.

Scoop.it is a content development site. You will find the best content on the web placed there, or *scooped*, by others. It has a good potential to increase your influence across the web, bring you mass blog traffic, help you meet like-minded, engaged bloggers, and offer you quality material to read on topics that interest you.

The articles you collect appear in a newspaper-style format. The name of the site is well suited because reporters get a "scoop" on new stories to cover.

KAPOST:

Kapost is a platform that takes into account every step of the content marketing cycle. One fantastic function is the ability to assign different pieces of content different buyer personas, which shows which stages of the content marketing cycle your prospects are the most likely to convert on.

Marketing success in today's digital world demands personalized experiences for prospects and customers who expect organizations to meet them exactly where they are in understanding, evaluating, and purchasing a product or service. That's not an easy task for modern B2B marketers who must navigate long and complex buying cycles, reach audiences through the dynamic digital channels in addition to offline channels, understand an increasingly complex technology landscape, provide data-driven insights to leadership, and collaborate across the many global teams—all while remaining on-message and on-brand.

Kapost is the solution to B2B marketing complexity. By enabling marketers to take control of the content operation with a single platform, Kapost brings complete visibility to content creation and performance at enterprise scale. From sharpening content strategy, to creating intelligent workflows, to measuring the impact of the content you create, Kapost is designed to help marketers truly master the trade and provide fine services to their customers. Building a content operation with Kapost complements marketing automation and CRM platforms and guides the optimization of people, processes, and technology to strategically plan, produce, distribute, and analyze content.

KISSMETRICS:

Kissmetrics offers analytics tools that help you increase conversions across your entire website. The platform tracks your site visitors throughout their entire conversion journey and gives you reports on each part of the funnel. This helps you fine-tune your entire conversion process to increase sales and revenue.

Kissmetrics is a kind of a behavioral analytics system. It assigns web site visitors unique IDs and then tracks things like their clicks, pages visited, 1-page visits followed by an exit, conversions. It does this over time and allows you to create segments for more effective and targeted marketing.

All of this is ultimately intended for improved threat and engagement measurement and better website personalization and conversion rates.

GOOGLE ANALYTICS:

Google Analytics is the gold standard for most websites these days. Google has advanced analytics that provide information on a variety of your website information, including who your visitors are, how they make their way to and through your sales funnel and what they do on your website in real-time.

The tool allows you to **track websites, blogs, and social networks.** In addition, it puts at your disposal predetermined and customizable reports. As indicated in its entry in Wikipedia, Analytics *"offers grouped information of the traffic that arrives at the websites according to the audience, the acquisition, the behavior, and the conversions carried out on the website."* **Google Analytics has lately been the dominant tool**. It offers more data and metrics than any other.

It works on elements as varied and vital as the following:

- Number of visits
- Their duration
- Sources of traffic
- Visited pages

It also acts on operations such as:

- Your users preferred sections
- Keywords used
- Technical details of visitors' devices.

But what makes Analytics a complete tool is its compatibility with the rest of Google's tools. Thus, it is possible to combine Analytics with AdWords, Blogger or YouTube. All Google tools in which visits and traffic are counted can be mixed and complemented with Google Analytics. In addition, there are different attractive resources for Analytics available in Google Chrome. You can work around with them too.

ADOBE ANALYTICS:

Adobe provides an enterprise-level analytics solution for companies who want to gather deep analytics on their website data and performance. The platform has cross-channel attribution functions, exhaustive customer analysis and predictive intelligence which enables you to observe and respond to customer actions in real time.

All Digital marketers and digital companies have a checklist for digital platform implementations and websites which is quite exhaustive but that contains two items for sure i.e. analytics and SEO. One of the best things about online marketing is that virtually everything is traceable so to tap into the benefits of analytics they jump onto implement a solution for their site. They end up paying full fees for Licenses and they rarely think about investing money for Analytics consultant which can help them tremendously by designing a solution for them.

Consultants know about all capabilities and what to do in certain business implementation. Adobe Analytics is the next generation interface that allows you to create a complete and distinguished view of your business by focusing on key character components.

WOOPRA:

Woopra is an analytics platform tailored for ecommerce businesses. Looking to help solve the problem of cart abandonment, Woopra analyzes each step of your site's checkout process to determine where visitors are dropping off and which traffic source is working the best in terms of checkout success.

Woopra works very much like Google Analytics – A tracking code is placed on your website which gathers information on every visitor which is then reported back to your Woopra Dashboard. For more advanced users, events can be created and triggered to identify users when they either login to your website or submit a contact form. You can then use al that information as you please to generate triggers.

ZENDESK:

Zendesk provides a full arsenal of tools that can get your support team up and respond to all of your customers' needs. The platform aggregates all of your communication channels into one place, which makes it simple to respond to your emails, phone calls and chats. Zendesk also integrates with Sprout, which streamlines the social customer service inputs.

Zendesk is a collection of support apps that helps transform your customer service into agents for customer retention and lead source. It has one of the most flexible plan structures, making it ideal for business of any size to afford packages that they need and can afford.

It consists of support, chat, call center solution and knowledge base modules that you can upgrade separately. However, its support plans include the basic versions of chat, call center and knowledge base, so you get all facets covered.

This setup affords a startup or small business to implement at once an industry-class help desk. They can easily upgrade to more advanced tools like CSAT surveys, web SDK, IVR phone trees and answer bot as their business requirements get complex.

Zendesk Support puts all customer interactions in one dynamic interface for an efficient and seamless process. You can bring in customer queries from almost any channel using pre-defined ticket responses, web widgets and customer search history, allowing you to respond faster and in the right context. The main module can also be customized to fit your customer service workflows or apps that you're already using. It also features customer satisfaction ratings and analytics via performance reports and dashboards.

The software also lets you develop institutional knowledge developed by your customer service over the years. The Guide module helps you build a help center, online community and customer portal. You can shoot FAQs and low-touch tickets to this portal, while your agents deal with high-value customers and leads.

Zendesk also gives you the option to set up a call center with web, mobile and messaging channels. This is ideal for highly engaged customers or prospects because your agents can quickly connect to them via an automated trigger. Through the integrated live chat, your agents can also proactively engage customers on your website or ecommerce page. You can also use analytics here to make sense of the conversations that are collected by your call center.

Overall, Zendesk is an extensive and focused help desk suite with all the essentials your support needs that you can scale according to your growth pace: ticketing system, knowledge base, community forums, live chat and call center.

USER VOICE HELPDESK:

UserVoice's a very professionally designed customer service platform and a great place for large teams to tackle online customer service needs. The reports offered make it easy to see which agents are performing the best, and customer satisfaction surveys let you know how your team performs as a team on the whole. Furthermore, the platform optimizes the process of collecting and analyzing customer feedback without interrupting your visitors.

LIVECHAT:

LiveChat takes a more proactive approach to customer service by facilitating conversations with the people visiting your website. The passive chat box that is placed on your page lets your potential customers reach right out to some of your service representatives, helping you effectively answer questions and queries.

Basically Live chat softwares use Web sockets to communicate across the servers.

In Layman's terms, Whenever you visit a website, you will have a *messenger option* which will help you talk to their operator. You must have seen them pop up on some websites you visit.

No need to call or wait for mail responses.

Now why people add it to website is something like this -

Serves customer on the go and *enhances the customer experience.*

Saving chat data makes *remarketing* easier. If you have proper keyword research than words used in chats can help in *SEO*.

Software also provides *reporting and analysis of the chats*. You can study client behaviors using this feature.

Frequently asked questions can be added to the knowledge base of the FAQ section for easy query solving.

Happy clients give following perks – revisits and backlinks.

SCREAMING FROG:

Screaming Frog is a spider tool that can quickly crawl through websites, lists of websites or specific web pages to give you a complete analysis of their performance. You can use the tool to see if you have any broken links, broken pages, bad redirects and much more. Fixing most of these errors is a real win for search marketers.

Screaming Frog is an essentially useful tool which can allow you to quickly identify issues your website might have. While this tool provides you with a large amount of data, it doesn't do the best job of explaining the implications of each item that it counts.

SEMRUSH:

SEMRush has a ton of built-in digital marketing tools that help both paid search experts and SEOs track and improve their search rankings. One major use of SEMRush is to track your competitors. You can use the tools to pull your competitor's backlinks, monitor their fluctuations in ranking and conduct a full competitive and comparative analysis.

SEMrush is a SEO tool that performs your keyword analysis, monitors your competition's keyword strategy, runs an SEO audit of your blog, looks for back linking opportunities to name a few.

SEMrush is trusted by internet marketers all over the world. It has a massive database of over 46 million domains and 120 million keywords. It tracks quite a few things, such as the organic position of a domain or landing URL on Google's SERPs, copies of AdWords ads and their positions, CPC ads, competitor analysis and so much more. It helps with your content marketing which is the most important thing it does.

SEMrush starts with free 30 days trial, however in the trial version we can use limited features. It offers 3 types of plans for its user who can go with it and choose the best one according to their business and budget. In just single dashboard we get everything done.

MOZ:

Moz offers two key products to customers: Moz Pro and Moz Local. The Moz Pro product helps with the classic SEO practices, such as tracking rankings, monitoring link building efforts and informing content marketing campaigns. Moz Local helps businesses improve their local SEO listings. All you need to do is enter your business's location information and Moz does the work of getting you listed.

Rand Fishkin and Gillian Muessig founded Moz in 2004 as an SEO focused company. Fishkin created Moz to help businesses integrate SEO into their digital marketing plans. Moz was started as a blog, called SEOmoz, for experts to share their research and ideas.

As SEOmoz became more popular, they turned into a full-fledged consulting firm. By 2013, SEOmoz rebranded as Moz and began focusing on providing SEO services and tools that help businesses grow.

Moz now offers software, educational videos, and community advice to help people become more proficient in SEO.

Moz Pro is an all in one tool that helps businesses manage numerous aspects of their SEO campaign. It's a great tool to use alongside Google Analytics. Moz Pro helps you understand your audience better. When visitors come to your site, you gain insight as to how they got there. You can see if they come from paid ads, search, or social media.

This tool helps you learn how people search for your business. You'll understand the keywords your audience uses to find your products or services better which can help you further with marketing your brand. When you know what your audience uses to find your business, you can use those keywords to attract more qualified leads to your page.

Local businesses rank differently in the search results than other businesses. Moz Local is Moz's other software that focuses on helping local businesses optimize their listing.

First, you need to verify your business listing with Google or Facebook. These local listings are a crucial part of SEO because it's eventually how your audience finds your business.

Once that's complete, Moz local completes your business listing. After your listing is prepared, Moz gets your listing ready for distribution and then distributes it across various search engines. These search engines display your site for the new customers to find.

With Moz Local, you can choose between two packages for local businesses.

Moz Local is a great option for small businesses with 1-99 locations. Moz Local makes it easy to optimize your business listing. They only make you fill out the data once for each location. The rest of the information is automated for you.

It sends the information to search engines and directories that your audience uses the most. The automation process makes it easy to make quick changes or fix errors across all your local listings. This prevents you from repeating work or duplicating listings hence saving on the budget and preventing from redundancy.

Moz Local is a great way to build trust with your audience. It helps you prevent from forgetting data or posting incorrect data. This increases your trust with search engines and gets them to see you as a legitimate local resource.

As a local business, reviews play a crucial role. With Moz Local, you'll get notifications when someone reviews your business on a popular site, which gives you the opportunity to reply promptly. It makes your business shine in a positive light.

DIFFERENT BUSINESS DEVELOPMENT STRATEGIES.

Throughout the book, I have stressed enough upon the miracles of business development, in fact that is what this book is about anyway!

But the best of the resources might fall flat on face if not planned and executed properly. Going about business development without proper strategies is still commonplace.

Therefore, a strategy needs to be in place. With a good strategy you can make anything work. You need to have an integrated plan to keep your audience engaged.

WHAT TO DO IF YOU DON'T HAVE A STRATEGY?

Start with a separate plan defining the alterations needed and making the report for changes in investment and changes in practices to your Business Development. Then, after receiving approval, create an integrated plan which is part of the overall plan, is fully aligned and becomes part of business as usual.

REASONS YOU NEED A STRATEGY.

1. *You're directionless*

    I find that companies without a digital strategy (and many that do) don't have a clear strategic goal for what they want to achieve online in terms of gaining new customers or building deeper relationships with existing ones. And if you don't have goals with SMART digital marketing objectives you likely don›t put enough resources to reach the goals and you don›t evaluate through analytics whether you›re achieving those goals.

2. *You won't know your online audience or market share*

    Customer demand for online services may be underestimated if you haven't researched enough about this. Perhaps, more importantly, you won't understand your online marketplace because the dynamics will be different to traditional channels with different types of customer profile and behavior, competitors, propositions, and options for marketing communications. There are great tools available from the main digital platforms where we can find out the degree of customer demand, You can do a search gap analysis using Google›s Keyword planner to see how you are tapping into the intent of searchers to attract them to your site, or see how many people interested in products or services or sector you could reach through Facebook IQ.

3. *Existing and start-up competitors will gain market share*

    If you're not devoting enough resources to digital marketing or you're using an ad-hoc approach with no clearly defined strategies, then your competitors will step upon you and run ahead.

4. *You don't have a powerful online value proposition to create*

    A clearly defined online customer value proposition tailored to your different target customer categories will help you differentiate your online service encouraging existing and new customers to engage initially and the stay loyal. Developing a competitive content marketing strategy is crucial to this for many organizations since the content is what engages your audiences through different channels like search, social, email marketing and on your blog.

5. *You don't know your online customers well enough*

    It's often said that digital is the "most measurable medium ever". But Google Analytics and similar will only tell you number of visits, not the behavior of visitors, what they think. You need to use other forms of website user feedback tools to identify your weak points and then address them to improve your business.

6. *You're disintegrated*

    It's all too common for digital marketing activities to be completed in solo whether that's a specialist digital marketer, sitting in IT or a separate digital agency. It's easier that way to package digital marketing into a convenient chunk but it's less effective. Everyone agrees that digital media work best when integrated with traditional media and response channels. It is always recommend to develop an integrated digital marketing strategy and once Digital Transformation is complete digital marketing activities will be part of your marketing plan and part of business as well.

7. *Digital doesn't have enough people or budget given its due importance*

   Insufficient resource will be devoted to both planning and executing e-marketing and there is likely to be a lack of specific specialist e-marketing skills which will make it difficult to respond to competitive threats effectively and immediately. This can eat into your business.

8. *You're wasting money and time through duplication and redundancy*

   Even if you do have sufficient resource it may be wasted due to lack of budgeting. This is particularly the case in larger companies where you see different parts of the marketing organization purchasing different tools or using different agencies for performing similar online marketing tasks and hence double spending on the same thing.

9. *You're not aware enough to catch up or stay ahead*

   If you look at the top online brands like Amazon, Dell, Google, Tesco, Zappos, they're all dynamic - trialing new approaches to gain or keep their online audiences. Take the cues and apply it to your business as well.

10. *You're not optimizing*

    Every company with a website will have analytics, but many senior managers don't ensure that their teams make or have the time to review and act on them. Once a strategy enables you to get the basics right, then you can progress to regular improvement of the key aspects like search marketing, site user experience, email and social media marketing.

HOW TO CREATE DIGITAL MARKETING STRATEGIES.

1. **Build your buyer personas.**

   For any marketing strategy -- offline or online -- you need to know who you're marketing to. The best digital marketing strategies are built upon detailed buyer personas, and your first step should be to create them.

   Buyer personas represent your ideal customer and can be created by researching, surveying, and interviewing your business's target audience. It's important to note that this information should be based upon real data wherever and whenever possible, as making assumptions about your audience can cause your marketing strategy to take the wrong direction.

To get a rounded picture of your persona, your research sample should pool all types of customers, prospects, and people outside your contacts database who align with your target audience.

But what kind of information should you gather for your own buyer persona to inform your digital marketing strategy? That depends on your businesses, and varies depending on whether you're B2B or B2C, or whether your product is high cost or low cost.

2. **Identify your goals and the digital marketing tools you'll need.**

   Your marketing goals should always be tied back to the fundamental goals of the business. For example, if your business›s goal is to increase online revenue by 10%, your goal as a marketer might be to generate 30% more leads via the website than you did last year to materialize that success that you want.

   Whatever your goal is, you need to know how to measure it, and more important is, actually be *able* to measure it. How you measure the effectiveness of your digital strategy will be different for each business and dependent on your goal, but it's important to ensure you're able to do so, as it's these metrics which will help you adjust your strategy in the future.

3. **Evaluate your existing digital channels and assets.**

   When considering your available digital marketing channels or assets to deploy into your strategy, it's helpful to first consider the bigger picture in order to avoid getting overwhelmed. The owned, earned, and paid media framework helps to categorize the digital vehicles, assets, or channels that you have already put to use.

   Owned Media

   This refers to the digital assets that your brand or company owns -- whether that's your website, social media profiles, blog content, or imagery, owned channels are the things your business has complete control over. This can include some off-site content that you own, but isn't hosted on your website, like a blog that you publish on Medium, for instance.

Earned Media

Quite simply, earned media refers to the marketing you've earned through word-of-mouth. Whether that's content you've distributed on other websites, PR work you've been doing, or the customer experience you've already delivered, earned media is the recognition you receive as a result of it all. You can earn media by getting press mentions, positive reviews, and by other people sharing your content on social media.

Paid Media

Paid media is a bit self-explanatory by what its name suggests and refers to any vehicle or channel that you spend money on to catch the attention of your buyer personas. This includes services like Google AdWords, paid social media posts, advertising, and any other medium for which you directly pay in exchange for visibility.

4. **Audit and plan your *owned* media campaigns.**

   At the center of digital marketing is your owned media, which is majorly the content. Every message your brand broadcasts can generally be classified as content, whether it's your About Us page, product descriptions, blog posts, eBooks, infographics, or social media posts.

   Content helps convert your website visitors into leads and customers, and helps to raise your brand's profile online -- and when it's optimized, it can also boost any efforts you have around the organic traffic. Whatever your goal, you're going to need to use owned content to design your digital marketing strategy.

   To build your digital marketing strategy, you need to decide what content is going to help you reach your goals. Take for instance, if your goal is to generate more leads via the website than you did last year, it's quite unlikely that your 'About Us' page is going to be of any use in the design of your strategy.

5. **Audit and plan your *earned* media campaigns.**

   Evaluating your previous earned media against your current goals can help you get an idea of where to focus your time. Look at where your traffic and leads are coming from and rank each earned media source from most effective to least effective and then deploy them in the same order.

You might find that a particular article you contributed to the industry press drove a lot of qualified traffic to your website, which in turn converted really well too. Or, you might discover that Facebook is where you see most people sharing your content, which in turn drives a lot of traffic.

The idea here is to build up a picture of what earned media will help you reach your goals, and what won't, based on historical data. However, if there's something new you want to try, don't just rule that out because it's not yet been tried and tested.

6. **Audit and plan your *paid* media campaigns.**

    This process involves much of the same process: You need to evaluate your existing paid media across each platform to figure out what's likely to help you meet your current goals.

    If you've been spending a lot of money on AdWords and haven't seen the results you had hoped for, maybe it's time to refine your approach, or rule it out altogether and focus on another platform that seems to be yielding better results.

    By the end of the process, you yourself should have a clear idea of which paid media platforms you want to continue using, and which you'd like to scrap from your strategy.

7. **Create your S.M.A.R.T. goals:**

    Use specific, measurable, achievable, realistic, and timely goals; also known as S.M.A.R.T. goals to guide your strategy. Think about your organization's short- and long-term goals for growth.

WHICH DIGITAL MARKETING STRATEGIES TO HAVE?

SEARCH ENGINE OPTIMISATION:

SEO is the process of improving your website so that it ranks highly in search engine results for keywords and phrases related to your business. The more keywords you rank for and the higher you rank the more people will see and become familiar with your website and business.

SEO aims to direct more traffic to your website from members of your target audience. These are consumers who are actively searching for the products and services you offer, as well as users searching for more top of the funnel content.

When it comes to digital marketing strategies, look at SEO as a requirement. It intercepts every member of your target audience no matter where they currently are in your sales funnel. The reason is that almost every user begins their search for a new product or service by looking up on a search engine.

PAY-PER-CLICK ADVERTISING:

PPC is a paid form of advertising that is a kind of an auction-based system.

With PPC, you bid on keywords that you want your ads to show up for. These ads then appear at the top of search results, above organic listings. If a user decides to click on your advertisement, you then have to pay for that click. In other words, you don't pay for ad space only for the results, so I think that is quite a cool thing.

PPC aims to reach searchers with transactional queries, meaning they're ready to buy your products or services. When they click on your ad, they'll arrive at your landing page and see a call-to-action to convert, whether by purchasing a product or signing up for an email newsletter.

For many businesses just getting started with digital marketing or looking for a quick boost, PPC is a useful online marketing strategy. It propels your website to the top of search results.

CONTENT MARKETING:

In content marketing, your business focuses on reaching, engaging, and connecting with consumers via content. This content, which can include videos, blog posts, infographics, and more, provides values to users. It's not, however, sales-orientated copy it's only informational.

The overall goal of content marketing as a digital media strategy is to provide valuable information to your target audience, increase traffic, and generate conversions. From a technical standpoint, content marketing also focuses on optimizing your content for search engines to improve your presence in search results.

In today's online marketplace, users have a lot of power. They can choose to read or ignore your company's messages, whether they're promotional or informational which is why content marketing is so essential now.

E-MAIL MARKETING:

Email marketing focuses on retaining existing customers, as well as gaining new ones. It's an excellent technique for building brand awareness, keeping your company on the top of the game, and encouraging repeat purchases.

A core part of email marketing is developing and refining your campaigns, as well as growing your audience. Like content marketing, email marketing also focuses on providing users with valuable information else why would people stay subscribed.

The idea is that, while these users may not need your services or products now, they'll likely remember your brand when it's time to make a purchase. That brand awareness encourages them to choose your company when they're ready to buy.

The main objective of email marketing as a digital marketing initiative is to stay in the memory for potential customers, and provide current clients with beneficial information, like relevant industry news, and personalized content, like product coupons, that will keep them coming back. When it comes to email marketing, it offers tons of benefits. That's why more than 80 percent of companies use email marketing, be it any kind of business from manufacturing operations to retail stores to technology businesses.

SOCIAL MEDIA MARKETING:

Social media marketing focuses on building brand awareness and increasing conversions. A social media marketing campaign can feature one or several social media platforms, depending on your target audience and their platform preferences.

The core goal of social media marketing is to increase brand awareness and conversions, as well as build and maintain your company's reputation. That is why social media marketing focuses on creating informational and promotional content while interacting with users on the various platforms.

Users rely on social media for more than sharing content with friends and family. They also use it for connecting with companies, whether by highlighting a positive shopping experience or purchasing a company's services.

If you're inactive on social media, you leave users with limited options for contacting your business which has a direct negative impact on your revenues. That is why having an active presence on social media is essential.

VIDEO MARKETING:

Using video marketing, your company increases its reach, grows its revenue, and expands its operations. Like content marketing, as well as email marketing, your business focuses on creating informational and valuable videos for its target audience.

No matter which types of videos you create, you're eventually trying to build brand awareness among your target audience. Like social media, email, and content marketing, this brand awareness can lead to valuable conversions later.

Video marketing focuses on improving brand awareness, conversion rates, and company revenue. It achieves these goals by creating valuable, high-quality content for users. This strategy, like voice search optimization, also appeals to current user behaviors.

With the ability to improve conversion rates, video marketing is becoming a go-to online marketing strategy. It's also a great addition to email marketing and content marketing, which both benefit from using videos.

VOICE SEARCH OPTIMISATION:

With voice search optimization, your company optimizes existing and new website content for voice search. The intention is to earn your website the featured snippet or higher spot in Google search results.

The goal of voice search optimization is to earn the featured snippet for keywords relevant to your target audience and business. By ranking for position zero, your company increases its online visibility to consumers which is beneficial to visits and in turn conversions.

With more people purchasing smartphones, as well as voice-activated speakers, voice search is becoming a new and popular way to search. It is quite in trend these days. As a result, it's one of the newest digital marketing strategies that companies should adopt.

Like email, consumers want promotional content from brands. They want to know about new products and offers on the existing ones, which is why investing in voice search optimization today can benefit your brand later, when voice-activated speakers provide these promotional options to companies.

HOW TO GET RICH BY AFFILIATE MARKETING?

Passive income excites people, does it not? It is one of the best ways to make money, because you are making money even while sleeping and as the name suggests, you can make all this money passively, without putting in any crazy effort.

Anyway, no one likes to wake up in the morning, go to office and work for someone else. The monotony and the rat race does take a toll on the mental well-being without really making you rich.

Affiliate marketing is one way where you can make large sums of money, sitting at the comfort of your home, or being anywhere in the world or while sleeping.

Affiliate marketing is an advertising model in which a company compensates third-party publishers to generate traffic or leads to the company's products and services. The third-party publishers are affiliates, and the commission fee incentivizes them to find ways to promote the company. The affiliate simply searches for a product they enjoy, then promotes that product and earns a piece of the profit from each sale they make for the brand. The sales are tracked via affiliate links from one website to another.

The Internet has increased the prominence of affiliate marketing. Amazon is the one to have popularized the practice by creating an affiliate marketing program whereby websites and bloggers put links to the Amazon page for a reviewed or discussed product to receive advertising fees when a purchase is made. In this sense, affiliate marketing is essentially a pay for performance marketing program where the act of selling is your source of income.

Affiliates redirect visitors who click on one of these links or ads to the e-commerce site. If they purchase the product or service, the e-commerce merchant credits the affiliate's account with the agreed-upon commission, which could be any percentage of the sales price.

The goal of using an affiliate marketer is to increase sales which is a win-win solution for the merchant and the affiliate.

Affiliate marketing is a popular tactic to drive sales and generate significant online revenue. Extremely beneficial to both brands and affiliate marketers, the new push towards less traditional marketing tactics has been quite successful. In fact:

- A large number of publishers leverage the power of affiliate marketing, a statistic that will continue to increase as affiliate marketing spending increases every year.

HOW DOES AFFILIATE MARKETING WORK?

Because affiliate marketing works by spreading the responsibilities of product marketing and creation across parties, it manages to leverage the abilities of a variety of individuals for a more effective marketing strategy while providing contributors with a share of the profit which is an incentive for them to promote the product more and better. To make this work, three different parties must be involved:

1. Seller and product creators.
2. The affiliate or advertiser.
3. The consumer.

Let's evaluate the complex relationship these three parties share to ensure affiliate marketing is a success.

1. **Seller and product creators.**

   The seller, whether a solo entrepreneur or a large enterprise, is a vendor, merchant, product creator, or retailer with a product to sell. The product can be a physical object, like household goods, or a service, like coaching classes. Also known as the brand, the seller does not need to be actively involved in the marketing, but they may also be the advertiser and profit from the revenue sharing associated with affiliate marketing.

2. **The affiliate or publisher.**

   Also known as a publisher, the affiliate can be either an individual or a company that markets the seller's product in an appealing way to potential consumers to increase sales. In other words, the affiliate promotes the product to convince consumers that it is valuable or beneficial to them and make them purchase the product. If the consumer does end up buying the product, the affiliate receives a portion of the revenue made which is pre-decided.

Affiliates often have a very specific audience to whom they market, generally sticking to that audience's preferances. This creates a defined niche or personal brand that helps the affiliate attract consumers who will be most likely to act on the promotion.

3. **The consumer.**

    Whether the consumer knows it or not, they are the principal makers of affiliate marketing. Affiliates share these products with them on social media, blogs, and websites.

    When consumers buy the product, the seller and the affiliate share the profits. Sometimes the affiliate will choose to be honest with the consumer by disclosing that they are receiving commission for the sales they make. Other times the consumer may be completely oblivious to the affiliate marketing operation behind their purchase.

HOW DO AFFILIATE MARKETERS GET PAID?

A quick and inexpensive method of making money without the hassle of actually selling a product, affiliate marketing has an attention from those looking to increase their income online.

1. **Pay per sale.**

    This is the standard affiliate marketing structure. In this program, the merchant pays the affiliate a percentage of the sale price of the product after the consumer purchases the product through the affiliate's marketing. In other words, the affiliate must actually get the investor to invest in the product before they will be compensated.

2. **Pay per lead.**

    A more complex system, pay per lead affiliate programs compensates the affiliate based on the conversion of leads. The affiliate must persuade the consumer to visit the merchant's website and complete the desired action which can be to either fill out a contact form, sign up for a trial of a product, subscribe to a newsletter, or download software or files.

3. **Pay per click.**

    This program focuses on incentivizing the affiliate to redirect consumers from their marketing platform to the seller's website.

This means the affiliate must engage the consumer to the extent that they will move from the affiliate's site to the seller's site. The affiliate is paid based on the increase in web traffic.

CHANNELS TO ENTER THE AFFILIATE MARKETING BUSINESS.

1. **Influencers.**

    An influencer is an individual who holds the power to impact the purchasing decisions of a large segment of the population. We had already discussed influencer marketing in detail so we already know how powerful the influencer are I the digital marketing chain. This person is in a great position to benefit from affiliate marketing. They already have impressive following, so it's easy for them to direct consumers to the seller's products through social media posts, blogs, and other enagements with their followers. The influencers then receive a share of the profits they helped to create.

2. **Bloggers.**

    With the ability to rank organically in search engine queries, bloggers are quite effective at increasing a seller's conversions. The blogger samples the product or service and then writes a comprehensive review that promotes the brand in a compelling way, driving traffic to the seller's site and increasing conversions.

    The blogger is compensated for his or her influence spreading the word about the value of the product and thus helping to improve the seller's sales.

3. **Paid search focused microsites.**

    Developing and monetizing microsites can also garner an impressive amount of sales. These sites are advertised within a partner site or on the sponsored listings of a search engine. They are different and segregated from the organization's main site. By offering more focused, relevant content to a specific audience, microsites lead to increased conversions due to their simple and straightforward call to action strategy.

4. **Email lists.**

    Despite its older origins, email marketing is still a viable source of affiliate marketing income. Some affiliates have email lists they can use to promote the seller's products. Others may leverage email newsletters that incorporate within them the hyperlinks to products, earning a commission after the consumer purchases the product. Another method is for the affiliate to build an email list over time. They use their various campaigns to collect emails and then send out emails regarding the products they are promoting.

5. **Large media websites.**

   Designed to create a huge amount of traffic at all times, these sites focus on building an audience of millions. These websites promote products to their massive audience through the use of banners and contextual affiliate links. This method offers better exposure and increased conversion rates, resulting in a handsome revenue for both the seller and the affiliate.

HOW TO BE A SUCCESSFUL AFFILIATE MARKETER.

1. **Develop a rapport.**

   When beginning your affiliate marketing career, you'll want to cultivate an audience that has very specific interests. This allows you to tailor your affiliate campaigns to their niche, increasing the likelihood that you'll convert a prospect into a customer. By establishing yourself as an expert in one area instead of promoting a large number of products, you'll be able to market to the people most likely to buy the product.

2. **Make it personal.**

   There is no shortage of products you'll be able to promote. You'll have the choice to pick and choose products that you personally believe in, so make sure that your campaigns center around truly valuable products that consumers will enjoy and not just sell any product for the sake of making that cash. You'll achieve an impressive conversion rate while simultaneously establishing the reliability of your personal brand.

   You'll also want to get really good at email outreach to work with other bloggers and influencers because collaborations can help you promote yourself too.

3. **Start reviewing products and services.**

    Focus on reviewing products and services that fall within your niche. Then, leveraging the rapport you have created with your audience and your reputation as an expert, tell your audience why they would benefit from purchasing the product or service you are promoting. Almost anything sold online can be reviewed if there is an affiliate program, you can review physical products, digital software, or even services booked online, like coachings or travel resort booking. It is especially effective to compare this product to others in the same category. Most importantly, make sure you are generating detailed, comprehensive content to improve conversions.

4. **Use several sources.**

    Instead of focusing on just an email campaign, also spend time making money with a blog, reaching out to your audience on social media, and even looking into cross-channel promotions. Test a variety of marketing strategies to see which one your audience responds to the most and the leverage on that strategy. Make frequent use of this technique.

5. **Choose campaigns with care.**

    No matter how good your marketing skills are, you'll make less money on a bad product than you will on a valuable one and choosing a bad product can also be detrimental to your reputation. Take the time to study the demand for a product before promoting it. Make sure to research the seller with care before collaborating. Your time is worth a lot, and you want to be sure you're spending it on a product that is profitable and a seller you can believe in.

6. **Stay current with trends.**

    There is serious competition in the affiliate marketing sphere. You'll want to make sure you stay on top of any new trends to ensure you remain competitive and are not left behind doing the same old things. Additionally, you'll likely be able to benefit from at least a few of the new marketing techniques that are constantly being created. Be sure you're keeping up to date on all these new strategies to guarantee that your conversion rates, and therefore revenue, will make you achieve your financial goals.

IMPORTANCE OF DROPSHIPPING.

Dropshipping is an order fulfillment method that does not require a business to keep products in stock. Instead, the store sells the product, and passes on the sales order to a third-party supplier, who then fulfills the order to the customer.

The biggest difference between dropshipping and the standard retail model is that the selling merchant doesn't stock or own inventory. Instead, the seller purchases inventory as needed from a third party usually a wholesaler or manufacturer to provide to the customers for the orders.

However, contrary to popular belief floating online, dropshipping is not a get-rich-quick scheme.

Sure, it seems like easy money — you sell other people's goods and take a cut for yourself — but when you factor in all the drawbacks, obstacles, and day-to-day management, it's a bit tricky.

BENEFITS OF DROPSHIPPING.

1. **Less capital is required.**

    Probably the biggest advantage to dropshipping is that it's possible to launch an ecommerce store without having to invest thousands of dollars in inventory up front. Traditionally, retailers have had to tie up huge amounts of capital purchasing inventory.

    With the dropshipping model, you don't have to purchase a product unless you've already made the sale and have been paid by the customer. Without significant up-front inventory investments, it's possible to start sourcing products and launch a successful dropshipping business even with very investment. And because you're not committed to selling-through any inventory purchased up front, like in a traditional retail business, there's less risk involved in starting a dropshipping store should you not make sales, no inventory will be dumped.

2. **Easy to get started**

    Running an ecommerce business is much easier when you don't have to deal with physical products. With dropshipping, you don't have to worry about managing or paying for a warehouse, packing and shipping your orders, tracking inventory for accounting reasons, handling returns and inbound shipments, continually ordering products and managing stock level

3. **Low overhead**

   Because you don't have to deal with purchasing inventory or managing a warehouse, your overhead expenses are quite low like the storage and shipping expenses. In fact, many successful dropshipping stores are run as home-based businesses, requiring a laptop and a few recurring expenses to operate. As you grow, these costs will likely increase but will still be low compared to those of traditional businesses.

4. **Flexible location**

   A dropshipping business can be run from just about anywhere with just an internet connection. As long as you can communicate with suppliers and customers easily, you can run and manage your business.

5. **Wide selection of products to sell**

   Since you don't have to pre-purchase the items you sell, you can offer an array of trending products to your potential customers. If suppliers stock an item, you can list it for sale on your online store at no additional cost.

6. **Easier to test**

   Dropshipping is a useful fulfillment method for both launching a new store and for business owners looking to test the demand that customers have for additional product categories, e.g., accessories or wholly new product lines. The main benefit of dropshipping is the ability to list and potentially sell products *before* committing to buying and storing a large amount of inventory.

7. **Easier to scale**

   With a traditional retail business, if you receive three times the number of orders, you'll usually need to do three times as much work. By leveraging dropshipping suppliers, most of the work to process additional orders will be borne by the suppliers, allowing you to expand with less incremental work.

Sales growth will always bring additional work—especially related to customer support—but businesses that utilize dropshipping, scale considerably well compared to traditional ecommerce businesses.

E-COMMERCE BUSINESS.

A few trillion dollars industry, e-commerce is really something people should already be tapping into.

eCommerce refers to any form of business transaction conducted online. The most popular example of eCommerce is online shopping, which is defined as buying and selling of goods via the internet on any device.

HOW TO START AN E-COMMERCE BUSINESS?

Research: Beginning your research is the first critical step. Don't operate off of a hunch. Growing any online business is an investment. Treat it so and you are bound to bear fruitful results.

Niche: Choosing your niche is the most important step in opening your online business. Start this process by identifying successful companies already working in this realm.

Make sure that the area is competitive an absence of competition might make it easier to sell but it also usually indicates that there's no market, either.

Don't pick an overly crowded niche or anything dominated by major brands. If you're having trouble with this, drill down further on what you want to do – the more specific you are, the less competition you are likely to face.

Niching down you can work together with business owners in those niches to cross-promote, become an affiliate, and grow your customer base.

Personas and Product Selection: Think about personas. You can't expect people to buy your product if you don't know who you're selling to. You can't expect to sell to audience A while targeting audience B. Once you've identified the image you want to project and the customer you are catering to, it's time to come up with product ideas.

MARKETING YOUR PRODUCTS ONLINE.

Your mission is to sell products, not just drive traffic. To sell products, you have to think beyond designing your site and look for expansion areas.

Providing consumers with coupons and content via email helps to keep your brand on their mind, boost sales, and establish credibility. Keep your emails interesting ask for your customers' input often especially reviews. Respond quickly to customer service and product quality issues, and work on building relationships. No sales interaction is about the first sale; focus on the next one always because losing customers can spread a bad name and you might end up losing business.

If you're driving traffic to your store but nothing is selling, fix the leaks in your sales funnel by carefully optimizing each page and taking a close look at your product listings. Use analytics to help with this task. There are tools that can help you monitor and optimize every step of the sales process. Make wise use of them.

Look into partner and affiliate marketing to boost your brand presence by offering affiliate marketing options and partnering with retailers in your shoulder niches.

ATTRACTING CUSTOMERS TO YOUR ONLINE STORE.

The keyword-stuffing days of the early 2000s are long gone, but SEO is alive and performing well. You need to keep keywords and search terms in mind on each page of your site, in your URLS, and in your ad campaigns. You also need to think about driving traffic to your site.

The best ecommerce sites are known to invest heavily in online marketing. Subscribe to marketing newsletters or listen to digital marketing podcasts to keep a pulse on the digital marketing industry and get your fill of marketing tips to use in boosting sales.

BENEFITS OF E-COMMERCE.

- **Global market.** A physical store will always be limited by a geographical area it can serve. An online store, or any other type of ecommerce business for that matter, has the whole world as its market. Going from a local customer base to a global market at no additional cost is really one of the greatest advantages of trading online.

- **Around-the-clock availability.** Another great benefit of running an online business is that it is always open. For a merchant, it's a dramatic increase in sales opportunities; for a customer, it's a convenient and immediately available option. Unbounded by the working hours, ecommerce businesses can serve customers 24/7/365, which makes it another brilliant source of passive income.

- **Reduced costs.** ecommerce businesses benefit from significantly lower costs required to run the business. As there's no need to hire sales staff or maintain a physical storefront, those running a drop shipping business enjoy even lower upfront investment requirements. As merchants are able to save on operational costs, they can offer better deals and discounts to their customers.

- **Inventory management.** ecommerce businesses can automate their inventory management by using electronic tools to accelerate ordering, delivery and payment procedures. It's saving businesses billions in operational and inventory costs.

- **Targeted marketing.** With access to such a valuable amount of customer data and an opportunity to keep an eye on customer buying habits as well as the emerging industry trends, ecommerce businesses can stay deft and shape their marketing efforts to provide a better and customized experience and find more new customers.

- **Serving niche markets.** Scaling a niche product to become popular is effortful. By tapping into a global market, ecommerce retailers can build a highly profitable niche business without any further investment. Using online search capabilities, customers from any corner of the world can find and purchase your products.

- **Working from anywhere.** Often, running an ecommerce business means that you don't need to sit in an office from 9 to 5 or suffer through a commute day-in and day-out. A laptop and a good internet connection is all it takes to manage your business from anywhere in the world. No traffic issues. No fixed hours. You become your own boss.

DEALING WITH CRITICISM AS A BUSINESS DEVELOPER?

To be successful is to be able to tackle difficult and uncomfortable situations, be headstrong and have a reasonably good Emotional Quotient.

A successful person has mastered the art of ignoring those people and those situations that do not serve them in their quest of success. They know that for one reason or another, someone will find a reason to project their insecurities, their negativity, and their fears onto you and your life, and you'll have to deal with it.

It doesn't matter how you choose to live your life whether you build a business or work a corporate job; have children or choose not to have children; travel the world or live in the same town all of your life; go to the gym 5 times a week or sit on the couch every night whatever you do, someone will judge you for it. There will always be haters and difficult people. Sadly, that is how the world functions.

Take what you must from the following to keep the negative energy at bay and not let those that don't cater to your needs bother you from getting ahead in life:

The Biggest Critic in Your Life

It's easier to complain about the outside critics, but the biggest critic in your life usually lives between your own two ears. Working up the courage to move past your own vulnerability and uncertainty is often the greatest challenge you'll face on the way to achieving your goals. And those that master this couldn't care less about what others have to say.

It is rarely the criticism from outsiders that holds you back. It is mostly your own mind worrying that people would think certain unpleasant thoughts about you and your choice in life.

It can take a lifetime to learn that just because people criticize you doesn't mean they really care about your choice to do something different. Usually, the haters simply criticize and move on. And that means that you can safely ignore them and continue doing your thing. It's okay if you steered away from a 9 to 5 job and it's okay if they don't understand what you are doing. As long as you get it, all is well.

But that is easier said than done because we all like to be validated. Some people like it more than others, but everyone wants to be respected and appreciated to some extent. I know that whenever we choose to take a risk and share our work with the world, we wonder about what our friends will think, what our family will think, and how the people around us will see us because of that choice. Will this help our reputation? Will this hurt our reputation? Should we even be worrying about our reputation?

The Truth About Criticism

Apparently, the tendency to hold onto negative criticism is natural for most people. We tend to remember negative emotions much more strongly and in more vivid detail.

Focus on the Road, Not the Wall

Criticism and negativity from difficult people is like a wall. And if you focus on it, then you'll run right into it. You'll get blocked by negative emotions, anger, and self-doubt. Your mind will go where your attention is focused. Criticism and negativity don't prevent you from reaching the finish line, but they can certainly distract you from it and is that any good anyway?

If you focus on the road in front of you and on moving forward, then you can safely speed past the walls and barriers that are around, you can even jump over those barriers.

When someone dishes out a negative comment, use that as a signal to go back to your work and to refocus on the road ahead of you. Some people take things personally and tear down the work of others to make themselves look better. Your life is too short to worry about pleasing those kind of people.

Lastly, I would like to sum up by saying that do not let people below you have a big effect and expensive opinions about your life. If you choose to respond to the haters, then surprise them with kindness. It won't affect your mental wellbeing which is the most important thing to achieve anything in life at all. Finally, and most importantly, make the choices that are right for you. People will criticize you either way.

MBA VERSUS BUSINESS DEVELOPMENT PROGRAMME

Money is the basic necessity of life and maybe you get oxygen to survive for free; money, you need to go out and earn for yourself. Now, there are two ways in which you can make money, either by doing a job or by being an entrepreneur; unless you want to steal.

People think that job is a safe option to pursue and is a comfortable way of life; wake up in the morning, go to the office, work for someone, come back in the evening and retire to sleep, wake up again and the next day and go through the same routine again and again for the rest of your life.

Is it really the most comfortable life? Wouldn't it grow monotonous. Anyway, who said there are no risks involved in jobs?

To get a job, you first need to get a degree. Without a degree no employer will even call you or an interview. To get a degree, you first need to go to a college, and given the infinite number of colleges, to get a valuable degree, you will need to get into a top ranked college, which is another task because there are admission tests and not everyone will get through the test.

Now, let us assume you got admission in that elusive course in the most coveted college, first of all there will be hundreds of people who got admission in the same college who are now your competition. Secondly, when you will go out in market with this degree, there will be people with more and better degrees and more experience. No matter how hard you try, there will always be someone better than you.

With so many people with so many degrees, do companies really have space to accommodate everyone? Only 10-20% of qualified people actively looking for job get employed, rest of them remain jobless and even become depressed.

Now, even if you get a job, what is the guarantee it is safe? Even if you perform to your fullest potential and give good results, if there is a slowdown, the company might fire you without giving you an explanation and again you become jobless.

Moreover, getting a degree is really expensive; not only are you spending so much money, which you will take years to recover, you are also losing on all the time you spend in getting that degree.

Your ultimate motto of doing a job was to make money. If we do the math; it will take you years to recover the money you invested in getting that degree. If you start working at 20 and retire at 60, you will have spent 40 years of your life working for someone else, putting in the hard work to make someone else's business successful and eventually, he is the one who will be making all the profits. What will you get? An annual increment of less than 10% while you work so hard to make their monthly turnover be more than your lifelong earnings.

Coming back to MBA, it is one of the most sought after degrees, one of the most expensive too. Most of the people who go to business schools are going with an intention to get a job, better than the one they had before; but a select few go to business schools to learn to do business. Really?

Do you really think after spending so much money on a degree that is designed to equip you with the skills of being an employee, you will be left with the investment and the mindset to start your own business?

To be an entrepreneur, you do not need to go to a business school. That course might be designed to teach you Business Administration but who is teaching that to you? An employee will be taking your classes and can an employee ever teach you to become an entrepreneur, how can he teach you something he has no experience in? Only an entrepreneur can teach you how to be an entrepreneur because he has been through the exact journey you are looking to embark upon.

As an MBA, you are being taught Business Administration but you are not given any product, the only product that you have is your degree. Now, if after learning all that you learnt in your course spanning 2 years, you come up with a brilliant Business idea, you have no funds left. In fact, most of you will have a loan to repay that will also have a heavy compound interest levied on it.

Even though, you've learnt Business Administration, you are still an employee of someone, working hard to make them successful.

If I compare it with the Business Development Program, as soon as you complete the program, you have a product on hand and that is the Business Development services that you can now provide to clients across the globe. Besides that, you will also be designated as a Business Developer. If you do not have an office in place as yet, you can even work from the comfort of your own home and make money from clients all over the world. You can either work as a freelancer or start a full-fledged company. The more you build other people's business, the more reputation you earn for your own and in return your own business flourishes. The best part is that you do not need to spend years and years in getting a degree. With focus and dedication, within 2-3 months, you can kick start your career as a Business Developer and start your journey towards your own million-dollars life.

But, it is not as easy as it sounds. Just learning the tools will never be sufficient. Just learning the tools will not fetch you clients. Just learning the tools with not make you an efficient and a successful business developer. You need to have a high emotional quotient, a high conviction, perseverance, ability to deal with pressure and leadership qualities. Not just to be a Business Developer, to be any kind of entrepreneur, you need to have these skills and if you are missing out on any of these or are unwilling to put in the hard work, you might as well be an employee or take the charge of your life, develop these skills, become an entrepreneur, retire early and enjoy a lifelong Financial Freedom.

www.ingramcontent.com/pod-product-compliance
Lightning Source LLC
Chambersburg PA
CBHW030939180526
45163CB00002B/637